Access to History
General Editor: Keith Randell

Edward VI and Mary:
A Mid-Tudor Crisis?

Nigel Heard

Hodder & Stoughton

LONDON SYDNE

Other titles in the series:

Luther and the German Reformation, 1517–55   ISBN 0 340 51808 1
Keith Randell

John Calvin and the Later Reformation   ISBN 0 340 52940 7
Keith Randell

The Catholic and Counter Reformations   ISBN 0 340 53495 8
Keith Randell

Spain: Rise and Decline, 1474–1643   ISBN 0 340 51807 3
Jill Kilsby

From Revolt to Independence: The Netherlands 1550–1650   ISBN 0 340 51803 0
Martyn Rady

British Library Cataloguing in Publication Data
Heard, Nigel
    Edward VI and Mary : a mid-Tudor crisis. – (Access to history).
    1. England, 1485–1603
    I. Title II. Series
    942.05

    ISBN 0 340 53560 1

First published 1990
Second impression 1991

Typeset by Wearside Tradespools, Fulwell, Sunderland
Printed in Great Britain for the educational publishing division of Hodder and Stoughton Ltd, Mill Road, Dunton Green, Sevenoaks, Kent by Page Bros, Norwich

Contents

Preface

To the general reader

Although the *Access to History* series has been designed with the needs of students studying the subject at higher examination levels very much in mind, it also has a great deal to offer the general reader. The main body of the text (i.e. ignoring the Study Guides at the ends of chapters) forms a readable and yet stimulating survey of a coherent topic as studied by historians. However, each author's aim has not merely been to provide a clear explanation of what happened in the past (to interest and inform): it has also been assumed that most readers wish to be stimulated into thinking further about the topic and to form opinions of their own about the significance of the events that are described and discussed (to be challenged). Thus, although no prior knowledge of the topic is expected on the reader's part, she or he is treated as an intelligent and thinking person throughout. The author tends to share ideas and possibilities with the reader, rather than passing on numbers of so-called 'historical truths'.

To the student reader

There are many ways in which the series can be used by students studying History at a higher level. It will, therefore, be worthwhile thinking about your own study strategy before you start your work on this book. Obviously, your strategy will vary depending on the aim you have in mind, and the time for study that is available to you.

If, for example, you want to acquire a general overview of the topic in the shortest possible time, the following approach will probably be the most effective:

1. Read Chapter 1 and think about its contents.
2. Read the 'Making notes' section at the end of Chapter 2 and decide whether it is necessary for you to read this chapter.
3. If it is, read the chapter, stopping at each heading or ★ to note down the main points that have been made.
4. Repeat stage 2 (and stage 3 where appropriate) for all the other chapters.

If, however, your aim is to gain a thorough grasp of the topic, taking however much time is necessary to do so, you may benefit from carrying out the same procedure with each chapter, as follows:

1. Read the chapter as fast as you can, and preferably at one sitting.
2. Study the flow diagram at the end of the chapter, ensuring that you understand the general 'shape' of what you have just read.
3. Read the 'Making notes' section (and the 'Answering essay

questions' section, if there is one) and decide what further work you need to do on the chapter. In particularly important sections of the book, this will involve reading the chapter a second time and stopping at each heading and * to think about (and to write a summary of) what you have just read.
4. Attempt the 'Source-based questions' section. It will sometimes be sufficient to think through your answers, but additional understanding will often be gained by forcing yourself to write them down.

When you have finished the main chapters of the book, study the 'Further Reading' section and decide what additional reading (if any) you will do on the topic.

This book has been designed to help make your studies both enjoyable and successful. If you can think of ways in which this could have been done more effectively, please write to tell me. In the meantime, I hope that you will gain greatly from your study of History.

Keith Randell

CHAPTER 1

A Crisis in Mid-Tudor England?

1 Introduction

The middle of the sixteenth century has often been seen as a 'dead' period between the exciting changes under Henry VIII and the consolidation and expansion of the reign of Elizabeth I. In part this is because the Whig historians of the nineteenth century did not see any great or 'progressive' events taking place in England at this time. They therefore regarded the reigns of Edward VI and Mary as unimportant. These Whig historians assumed that events were shaped by 'great' men (or women). This attitude has created the traditional view of the period, and the years between 1547 and 1558 have tended to be seen in terms of personalities rather than events. The major and tragic figures have been the dying boy king and the haunted, half-Spanish Mary, driven by love for Philip II and the Catholic religion to commit atrocities against her Protestant subjects. In the background have lurked the obscure and slightly sinister figures of the Lord Protector Somerset and the Lord President Northumberland, one provoking popular rebellion and the other plotting to seize the Crown. These were the people who were thought to have created history and little attention was given to the mass of the population, or to the underlying issues which shaped events.

Over the last 40 years historians have changed their views about the mid-sixteenth century, and much research has been carried out to show that it marked a significant turning-point in English history. Although historians are agreed that the period was significant, they are certainly not in agreement as to the way in which it was important. Most historians concur that it was a time of potential crisis, but there is a wide disparity of views over both the cause and the nature of any such crisis. There are two broad schools of historians – revisionist and Marxist. Not only are the two groups mutually opposed, but members of both schools disagree among themselves. The revisionists largely interpret events in terms of the constitution, politics and changes among the ruling élites, while Marxist historians tend to create general theories based on long-term changes in the economy and society. Consequently, the range of conflicting evidence and theory becomes increasingly difficult to master. This makes it essential for the student to create a broad framework within which to study the period. The easiest way to do this is to divide the events into four categories: political, religious, social and economic, and to set the events against two broad interpretive concepts: the rise of the State, and the theory of crisis. While dividing things up in this manner makes it much easier to generalise, it is important to remember that the political, religious, social and economic events are all closely inter-related, and that the two interpretive concepts of 'the State' and 'crisis' are interlocking.

* Just as it is essential for the student to be able to set events in a clear framework or context, it is equally necessary to establish a firm grasp of the causes of the events and of their consequences. In doing this, care must be taken to distinguish between long and short-term causes and to decide whether the events themselves are significant over a long period, or whether they have only immediate consequences. This is particularly important when considering the changing and differing theories of crisis and applying them to England in the middle of the sixteenth century. Most revisionist and Marxist historians use these theories to explain the various problems experienced by western European countries in the sixteenth and seventeenth centuries. However, it must be remembered that the so-called mid-sixteenth-century crisis did not form part of a general European crisis in the same way as did those of the late fourteenth and early seventeenth centuries. It was confined to England. In any case, historians are now becoming suspicious of theories of general crisis, and are coming to the view that history should be seen in terms of separate crises occurring in individual countries at different times.

A major difficulty for the student trying to use any theory of crisis is to decide what is meant by the term. By definition a crisis is a brief moment of danger. So how long can a crisis last – a few months, a year, or a number of years? In the latter case, it is possible to see the whole period from 1547 to 1558 as a crisis, but it might be more realistic to see years of particular danger – 1547, 1549 and 1553 – as the real crisis points in England. Clearly this raises the question of what creates a crisis. It can be said that a crisis results from an immediate short-term problem such as a foreign invasion, a rebellion or a harvest failure. Equally it can be maintained that a crisis is created by a combination of long-term problems which together threaten the collapse of government or the State. The problems in England during the reigns of Edward VI and Mary combine all these possibilities. Yet, even so, it has to be decided whether the English State was in serious danger of collapse.

* Even before trying to answer this question it is necessary to establish exactly what is meant by the sixteenth-century State. Revisionist and Marxist historians are generally agreed that the feudal crisis and chronic anarchy of the late Middle Ages enabled western European monarchs to gain power at the expense of the Church and the aristocracy. There is broad agreement that those monarchs who were able to take advantage of this situation increased their power and became the centrepiece of a new type of State. They achieved this by creating permanent central and local bureaucracies dependent on royal patronage, and by controlling military power. At the same time these

See Preface for explanation of * symbol.

monarchs had to maintain a balance between the various sections of their subjects by gaining their acceptance of the legitimacy of royal authority. The main difference in approach between historians is that while the revisionists are more concerned with the political and constitutional developments within the State, Marxists stress the economic role of the State in the growth of a capitalist system. Thus when historians of either school discuss the sixteenth-century State they are visualising it as the monarch and the permanent machinery of central and local government through which he or she and his or her advisers ran the country.

It is now generally accepted that, within this broad framework, the states of western Europe were created and developed along different lines depending on their geographical, religious, social, political and economic background. Unlike 'absolutist' states on the continent where, theoretically, the monarch was above the law, had independent sources of taxation and controlled paid officials and mercenary armies, England was a constitutional monarchy. English monarchs were answerable to Parliament and had to rule through Statute law. At the same time they had to rely on the revenue from royal estates, and whatever money they could persuade Parliament to grant them. In turn this meant that they could rarely afford to keep a standing army of mercenaries and had to rely on the goodwill of the aristocracy and gentry to raise troops from among their tenants. Shortage of money also meant that they depended on these same landlords to act as an unpaid bureaucracy to run local government – as Justices of the Peace for instance. While this might seem to indicate that the English State was in a weaker position than its more authoritarian counterparts on the continent, some historians suggest that the other side of the coin was just as important: that the English taxpayer was getting government on the cheap and was therefore less likely to rebel.

Order was the central problem for the sixteenth-century State. Monarchs had to raise money for the ever-increasing machinery of government needed to maintain peace and security, manage the economy and create social harmony. To achieve this they had to increase their revenue, but extra taxation was unpopular and likely to provoke rebellion, so leading to the collapse of government. English monarchs depended on the active support of the majority of landowners and the 'bourgeoisie' (defined by Marxist historians as the rising commercial and professional middling group in society), and on the passive obedience of the great mass of the population who had no share in the running of the country. Anything that upset this delicate balance could create a crisis for the English State, if not necessarily for the English people.

In terms of these broad theories the death of Henry VIII in 1547 presented England with a whole series of problems. Although Henry had made careful provision for the succession of his young son Edward, the prospect of a minority posed a serious threat to the stability of the government, particularly as the factions at Court were deeply divided over religious issues. This certainly represented a potential crisis for the State, which might have led to civil war, or invasion by a foreign power to restore the Catholic religion. As well as these political and constitutional difficulties, England faced a number of long-term socio-economic problems. By the beginning of the sixteenth century the English population had begun to recover from the worst effects of the Black Death and the subsequent plague cycle. Rising population forced up rents and food prices and made it difficult to find work, causing distress among the urban and rural poor. These difficulties were made worse in the middle of the century by the collapse of the English cloth trade which threw large numbers of people out of work. Popular unrest was increased by the rapidity of religious changes between 1547 and 1550, as many people felt that their old, traditional way of life was under threat. This was reflected in the growing tension between the mass of the small peasant farmers and the yeomen and gentry, as the peasants felt that the latter were using the commercial and religious situation to their own advantage. So by 1547 England seemed to be in a precarious position with possible conflict among the ruling élites, the threat of foreign invasion, a failing economy and rising popular discontent. These are the issues to be re-examined to see if all, or any, of them represented a 'mid-Tudor crisis'.

2 A Crisis of the State: Politics, Religion and Foreign Policy

Historians consider that after the English Reformation, religion had a significant effect on both politics and foreign policy. In recent years there have been many revisions of the interpretation of the events in England in the mid-sixteenth century which add to the difficulties of the student studying the period for the first time. This makes it essential to maintain a sense of balance; to be able to divide events up into manageable sections while preserving the wider perspective, by being able to see the essential inter-relationship between the events. Although this sounds a daunting task, it is fortunate that the concept of the State provides an easy and convenient connecting link.

By the early sixteenth century the State was assuming greater responsibility for every aspect of life. In much of Europe government was becoming centralised in capital cities such as London, and growing numbers of civil servants were being employed to administer both central and local affairs. At the same time the State was trying to take control in areas where it had had little or no influence during the Middle Ages. As the administration grew in size, statesmen realised that they had to take more control of the economy to ensure that the country was creating the wealth needed to pay the cost of government. Consequently the State began to pass legislation to try (often without success) to regulate the economy, and place restrictions on the way in which individual merchants and industrialists could operate. Many European countries, including Catholic ones, were deciding that religion was such a fundamental concern that it could no longer be left under the control of the Pope in Rome. In England the Henrician Reformation of the 1530s had made the monarch Head of the Church and given Parliament control of religious policy. This meant that religion had become part of the State's social policy, by which the government tried to maintain stability and cohesion. Yet, while the English State had gained great power and influence, it was becoming recognised that the government was responsible for the welfare of all the people in the country. Not only was the State expected to help the poor by taking over the charitable work previously carried out by the monasteries, but, also, to find employment for all the able-bodied.

Most historians accept this broad picture of the English State. Although it may appear very much like the creation of the twentieth-century historians using hindsight, it was precisely in these terms that the people of sixteenth-century England saw it as well. The Commonwealth, or 'commonweal' was a nationalistic and patriotic concept, but at the same time it contained the idea that the government was responsible for the welfare of all citizens, just as all citizens had the obligation to serve the State. This is well expressed by John Pym:

1 The form of government is that which doth actuate and dispose
 every member of a state to the common good; and as those parts
 give strength and ornament to the whole, so they receive from it
 again strength and protection in their several stations and de-
5 grees. If this mutual relation and intercourse be broken, the
 whole frame will quickly be dissolved, and fall to pieces.

Although this was written in the 1620s, Pym is describing what he saw as the good and well-balanced Parliamentary constitution and government of the sixteenth century. Of course, this was an idealistic view of government and society, which only worked partially and for some of the time. The government found it difficult to see all the connections between different parts of the framework. Individuals at all levels of society, like modern historians, had their own biases and priorities. The sixteenth-century English State could only function with the consent of a majority of the people, and the art of government was to achieve as much as was practicable in the circumstances.

*Crucial to the delicate structure of checks and balances was the monarch. Although the State was growing in power and becoming more stable with the development of new offices of state and permanent civil servants, it was still dependent upon the personality of the king or queen. Much of the thinking behind the duties of the State was paternalistic. Just as a father was head of a family and was responsible for the well-being of the family, so the monarch was to the nation. Equally, just as the father expected obedience from all members of the family, so the monarch expected unswerving loyalty from his subjects. The relationship between the monarch and his people and his place within the State is clearly shown in the Treason Act of 1547:

1 Nothing being more godly, more sure, more to be wished and desired, betwict a Prince the Supreme Head and Ruler and the subjects whose governor and head he is, than on the Prince's part great clemancy and indulgency . . . and on the subject's behalf
5 that they should obey rather for . . . love of a king and prince, than for fear of his strait and severe laws; yet such times at some time cometh in the commonwealth that it is necessary and expedient for the repressing of the insolency and unruliness of men and for the forseeing and providing of remedies against
10 rebellion . . .

Here is another view of the State which is very similar to John Pym's idealistic picture of the sixteenth-century constitution. Edward VI, although only nine years old, is seen as the father of his people. It is a relationship based on mutual cooperation and love, but the king, like a father, has to punish his children if they become fractious. In mid-sixteenth-century England the king was seen in these paternalistic terms, and was regarded as the keystone of the constitution.

Such paternalistic attitudes meant that many of the ruling élites thought the monarch should be male. Many continental countries recognised Salic Law, which excluded women from succession to the throne. Although England did not do this, there was no tradition of female monarchs. Henry VIII's anxiety to beget a male heir seems to suggest that he considered that a female heir presumptive would create dynastic weakness. When Edward VI died in 1553, the Lord President Northumberland tried to exclude the princesses Mary and Elizabeth from the throne because they were regarded as illegitimate, and, because as women, they might endanger the security of the State by marrying foreign princes (see page 36). Instead he attempted to strengthen his own control over the Crown by replacing them with another woman, Lady Jane Grey, who was married to his eldest son. Although Northumberland was unsuccessful it is clear that Mary, after she had overthrown him in 1553, was conscious that there was opposition to the idea of a female monarch, especially one who was unmarried. In 1554 Parliament passed an Act Concerning Regal Power which made it very clear that, within the English constitution, royal authority was 'invested either in male or female, and are and ought to be taken in one as in the other'. Some constitutional historians see this as a very significant piece of legislation, which, by removing doubts about the right of women to rule in England, prevented constitutional

Edward VI and his Council, from a woodcut on the Title to the Acts of Parliament 1551

crises in the future. For other historians, however, the crucial point concerning the succession was not one of sex, but the question of age and ability.

*Most historians agree that if there was to be a constitutional crisis in mid-sixteenth-century England, it was likely to be caused by the succession of the nine-year-old prince Edward. There is little doubt that England in 1547 could have seen a return to the chaos of the feudal anarchy of the Wars of the Roses in the second half of the fifteenth century. That there was no real crisis in either 1547 or 1553 is seen to be the result of the loyalty and support of the majority of the population for the process of legitimacy and law. The fact that the succession of a minor in 1547 did not cause an immediate crisis does not lessen the potential gravity of the situation. Historians are in broad agreement that a central feature in the development of the State was the struggle for power among the ruling élites. In such circumstances a strong, adult monarch was needed to maintain control, and the accession of a nine-year-old minor clearly opened the way for ambitious men to attempt to gain power.

Revisionist historians see this power struggle as taking two main forms. At the Court, the centre of government, the courtiers formed groups, or factions, which were constantly striving to gain royal favour.

This is not considered to have been particularly dangerous, because factions are seen as a normal part of Tudor government. A much greater threat is seen to be the rivalry between the 'court' and 'country' parties – although neither were political parties in the modern sense of the term. The 'court party' is seen as consisting of the members of the Privy Council, government officers and courtiers, all of whom held office and enjoyed royal patronage. The 'country party' was made up of those among the élites who did not hold office or enjoy royal favour, and generally lived on their estates in the countryside. Members of the 'country party' are seen as resenting the growth of the central bureaucracy because they thought it was sucking power and wealth into London at the expense of the provinces. The extent to which such a situation had developed by the mid-sixteenth century is uncertain, but the hostility displayed towards Somerset and Northumberland by many of their fellow members of the élites can be seen as part of this process.

Marxist historians see this struggle for power as part of the class conflict between the old aristocracy and the rising commercial and professional groupings drawn from town and country. Twenty years ago it was fashionable to describe this in terms of 'the rise of the middle class' – a conflict between the new, commercially-oriented smaller landowners, merchants and professional men, and the old military aristocracy for the control of central and local government. Now it is agreed that these distinctions are much less clear-cut, and that it is often difficult to show the difference between merchants, rising gentry, and the old aristocracy. Most Marxist historians are now willing to agree that the conflict was between active reformers and conservatives, who were drawn equally from the ranks of the aristocracy and the new rising groups. This can be seen as the beginning of a struggle for power between Protestant capitalist interests and the conservative, Catholic forces of paternalism.

*Historians see foreign policy as central to the political development of the State. It is generally agreed that the major problem for the new states was to find fresh sources of revenue to meet their rising costs. Increased taxation was unpopular and might lead to rebellion, while borrowing, or debasement of the coinage, was equally dangerous and might result in bankruptcy or high inflation, which merely added to the cost of government. The alternative was for the State to adopt an aggressive foreign policy to acquire land, wealth and trade. Unfortunately warfare was extremely expensive, particularly because of the rapid changes in military technology. As a result a country waging war, even a successful one, might bankrupt itself.

By the middle of the sixteenth century England was neither strong nor wealthy enough to compete with the great continental powers such as the Holy Roman Empire, or France. This meant that it was necessary for England to ally with one or other of her more powerful neighbours. Until 1559 western European foreign policy was dominated by the conflict between the Valois kings of France and the Habsburg rulers of the Empire and Spain. Several diplomatic considerations made it natural for the early Tudors to ally themselves with the Habsburgs. France had been England's national enemy throughout the Middle Ages. Henry VIII's marriage to Catherine of Aragon in 1509 linked England dynastically with Spain and the Empire. This alliance not only offered more protection against possible French aggression, but it was hoped it might also help the English kings to regain their territories lost to France by the end of the Hundred Years War. Another important consideration was that the Habsburgs ruled the Netherlands, the major industrial centre in northern Europe. As the English economy was dependent on the export of cloth to the Netherlands, it was essential to maintain good Anglo-Habsburg relations. Although the English Reformation of the 1530s soured connections with the Catholic lands and Spain, the Anglo-Habsburg alliance was maintained until the death of Mary in 1558.

These issues will be discussed in greater detail in Chapters 2, 3 and 4.

3 A Crisis of the State: Social, Religious and Economic Change

All social and economic historians are agreed that fundamental structural changes were taking place in western Europe in the sixteenth century and that these changes were the result of the crisis in the late medieval economy. However, they do not agree on the causes of the fourteenth-century 'feudal' crisis or on the nature of the changes taking place. Much of the research which has led to this re-interpretation has been based on England. Despite differing opinions over detail, it is generally agreed that the underlying structural change taking place here was a movement away from a peasant, self-sufficient economy towards a commercial market economy.

Marxist historians see the 'feudal' crisis in terms of a dramatic breakdown in the relationships between peasant tenants and their landlords, resulting in a change from a feudal 'mode of production' to a capitalist 'mode of production'. They argue that the feudal mode was a set of relationships which governed the medieval economy. Production was controlled by peasant farmers who not only provided food for consumption by their own families but, also, the food to support the clergy and the military and administrative élites. This process is called 'surplus extraction' and the extra food was collected through taxes, tithes and rents. These great landlords, it is claimed, spent their income on luxury goods, warfare and castle-building, and as costs increased they had to raise rents, tithes and taxes – a process called 'extra surplus extraction'. As the landlords did not invest their money to improve the efficiency of their estates by improving the quality of their land or introducing new farming techniques, the soil became exhausted and the level of food production fell. By the end of the Middle Ages there was growing resentment among the peasantry who were faced by falling crop yields and rising rents. They began to abandon their farms, to refuse to pay rents and to stage rebellions. Such peasant resistance forced the great landlords to lease out their land in larger units to commercial farmers, and this resulted in more peasants being forced off the land to work for wages in agriculture and industry. This was the new and more exploitative 'mode of production', based on wages, which was spreading in England during the sixteenth century. In turn, this new form of economic relationship caused further resentment, leading to class conflict between the wage-earners and the commercial 'bourgeoisie' in both town and country.

While non-Marxist historians agree that these changes took place, they account for them very differently and see no evidence for class conflict. For them the late medieval crisis came as a result of drastic changes in the level of population. By the end of the thirteenth century the population growth during the Middle Ages had put great pressure on land and food supplies. This population pressure, combined with inefficient farming techniques, had led to soil exhaustion and a 'Malthusian' crisis – when population outstrips food production and results in famine. The Black Death of 1349 solved this problem by reducing the population by about a third. Further outbreaks of bubonic plague maintained a high death rate, so that the population of England had been reduced from about six million in 1300 to about one and a half million by the middle of the fifteenth century. Such a drastic loss of population led to a deep recession which caused a sharp reduction in food prices and rents, but created a demand for labour. As a result, wages rose. While this was very advantageous to the peasants and wage labourers it was disastrous for the great landowners, who lost income from rents and the sale of foodstuffs. Furthermore, they had great difficulty in finding tenants among the peasantry, especially as many of the smallholders found it more profitable to leave their farms to work for wages. The great landowners were left with no alternative but to rent out all their land cheaply on long leases of up to 99 years to ambitious members of the gentry and prosperous peasant farmers, or yeomen. When the population began to recover by 1500 these commercially-oriented gentry and yeomen benefited from the rise in food prices and rent levels, while themselves enjoying low rents because of the long leases obtained in the fifteenth century. The great landowners could not benefit from the upturn in the economy until the long leases ran out in the second part of the sixteenth century, while the peasantry suffered from rising rents, and the wage-earners from increased food prices. The consequence was the rise of these new commercial groups at the expense of the great landowners, the peasantry and the wage-earners. The peasantry and the wage labourers, looking back on what for them was the 'golden age' of the fifteenth century, resented these changes, and this was to be the cause of popular unrest during the sixteenth century.

*Whichever of these long-term explanations of change (or whatever combination of them) is accepted, the result was the creation of fundamental structural shifts in England. By the middle of the sixteenth century the government was beginning to face severe economic problems. The population had risen to 2.3 million by the 1520s and had possibly increased to over 3 million by 1550. This necessitated feeding the extra people – a difficulty made worse because of the number of former peasants who left the land to live in the towns which were dependent upon the countryside for food. Many historians consider that the large number of self-sufficient peasant farmers still remaining also made the situation worse. Not only were their traditional methods of family farming not very efficient, but their presence prevented their land from being farmed commercially. This can be seen as the basic crisis of mid-century English farming: commercial expansion being severely limited by peasant self-sufficiency. However, there is little evidence that the commercial farmers were very successful in increasing the levels of food production. Although some new methods were introduced and farming became more specialised – particularly near large towns such as London – many of the gentry and yeomen up to 1550 were more interested in sheep farming in order to benefit from high wool prices. To improve efficiency and increase production many of the commercial farmers fenced off their land from the old open fields. This was the cause of many of the complaints about enclosure of land and the eviction of peasants, particularly when former arable land was converted to pasture. Yet it was necessary to create compact farms and to fence in the common land to bring it under cultivation if farming was to become more specialised and productive. Such was the dilemma facing the government, and by the late 1540s a series of bad harvests and growing shortages showed that population was once again outstripping food supply.

Quite apart from the potential dangers of another 'Malthusian' crisis in the mid-sixteenth century, this situation can be interpreted as presenting a long-term social problem for the government; a position made worse by recurring economic crises. The government aimed to maintain social stability and order, while, at the same time, accepting increased responsibility for poor relief and welfare. The government did not wish to see the peasant smallholders evicted or forced to leave the land because they would either drift into the towns or become vagrants, providing a possible source of riot and unrest. Enclosures were seen as the major cause of economic problems and social instability, and the government tried to pass laws against the practice. The difficulty was that Parliament, representing the landed interests, often blocked such legislation. Even when anti-enclosure laws were passed, the local magistrates (who were landowners themselves) frequently refused to enforce them. Consequently, not only did the State show itself to be incapable of taking effective action, but it antagonised the landowners by trying to prevent enclosure, and the peasantry by not preventing it.

Although in the sixteenth century most people lived on the land and depended on agriculture for a livelihood, an increasing minority of the people dwelt in towns and were employed in industry. Here again the State encountered severe difficulties. Most historians would agree that there was an urban crisis in the sixteenth century, and that by 1550 there was danger of industrial collapse. Once again the long-term causes of this situation can be traced back to the late Middle Ages. Early medieval industry was carried out in the towns and was controlled by craft guilds. The largest industry was clothmaking but output was on a small scale: most of the goods manufactured were sold locally. The major international export was wool, which was sold mainly to the Netherlands and Italy. By the thirteenth century many merchants and industrialists were beginning to leave the towns because of restrictive guild regulations and the high cost of urban overheads. The result was the establishment of a commercial rural cloth industry, based on the 'putting-out' system. It produced large quantities of semi-manufactured cloth which were exported to the Netherlands for finishing and sale. The new industry, based in East Anglia and the West Country, continued to expand during the recession of the fifteenth century. This encouraged landowners to convert arable land into sheep pasture to meet the ever-increasing demand for wool. The transfer of the cloth industry to the countryside caused problems for many towns, and these were made worse by the recession during the late Middle Ages. In addition, because of the very high urban death rate, towns were dependent upon migrants from the countryside to maintain, or increase, their population level. The sharp decline in national population during most of the fifteenth century reduced the flow of migrants, and many towns began to shrink in size.

When population levels began to recover c 1500, people who could not find work in the countryside drifted into the towns. Consequently, many towns were faced with a new problem of having too many migrants and were unable to feed, house, or employ them. In addition, the number of migrants increased because the country-based textile industry was facing growing competition from new types of cloth made on the continent. This meant that from the 1520s there were frequent slumps in demand, and many laid-off workers were forced to go to the nearest town to seek work. By 1550 the Antwerp market had slumped, causing widespread unemployment among English clothworkers. Other sources of work were scarce. Although many people were leaving the land and were available for employment in industry, there was little investment in towns to create new jobs. Consequently, the towns faced a very real crisis. The urban authorities had to contend with the problem of housing and feeding large numbers of unskilled migrants with little prospect of finding employment for them. By the mid-sixteenth century the government was threatened by rising discontent in both towns and countryside. The poor agricultural performance meant that the towns had great difficulty in feeding their rising populations and this created the threat of serious bread and unemployment riots. The situation was no better in the countryside. Discontent over enclosures and rising rents was increased by the loss of employment in the rural cloth industry on which many of the agricultural poor relied for subsistence. In these circumstances it is hardly surprising that the Lord Protector Somerset was confronted by widespread popular uprisings in 1549.

    *To a large extent these economic problems were outside the control of the mid-Tudor government. To meet the increasing cost of the administration and expand the national economy the English State needed to find new markets both in and beyond Europe to raise national wealth. The exploration carried out by Spain and Portugal in the fifteenth century is seen as part of this general process of State development. Yet while Spain and Portugal were gaining new markets, colonies and raw materials and France and the Empire were growing in strength, England was preoccupied with civil war.

    Far from gaining new territories and trade, she lost all her continental markets apart from the Netherlands. Only the new western European nation states had enough power and wealth to develop oceanic trade and to establish colonies in the New World. Many historians see this process of developing long-distance, world trade as essential to the growth of the new, centralised states and the expansion of western capitalism based upon the principle of economic growth. The opening up of the new sea routes to the Far East and America began to shift the economic centre of western Europe away from the Mediterranean and towards north-western Europe. This Atlantic economy was eventually to be dominated by states such as France, Holland and England, while, despite their early colonial exploration and monopoly of the world trade, southern European countries such as Spain and Portugal increasingly became economic backwaters. Clearly, in order to overcome her economic problems England needed to participate in world trade to gain the raw materials and markets to stimulate demand and create new jobs. The first two Tudor monarchs, however, showed little interest in Atlantic trade. Henry VIII in particular was much more concerned with his continental ambitions. In any case, England at this stage could not afford to antagonise her Habsburg allies by breaking their monopoly of the American trade. Not until after 1550, with the collapse of the Antwerp market, was the English government forced to show any serious interest in colonial exploration and the establishment of new markets.

    The emergence of this new economic system is seen by many

historians as being linked with the development of Protestantism. It has been suggested that it was significant that the north-western countries which were to dominate world trade were all strongly influenced by Protestantism, and especially Calvinism, while the more economically backward countries were all Catholic. Consequently the conflicts between the countries of the Reformation and the Counter Reformation can be interpreted as economic wars just as much as wars of religion. The reason for this economic divergence is seen to be the result of different social structures in Protestant and Catholic countries. The Protestant work ethic, it is claimed, encouraged thrift, hard work and commercial enterprise, while the Catholic religion was opposed to money-making and competition. The result was the continuation of traditional, self-sufficient peasant economies in the Mediterranean countries, while more progressive social economies based on wage labour developed in north-west Europe. Although it is widely agreed that such explanations are too simplistic to be totally acceptable, they still play an important part in interpretations of western capitalism. Despite the fact that by 1550 England remained a backward, off-shore European island and was not to take any significant part in world trade until the end of the sixteenth century, many historians accept the economic and religious changes taking place as an explanation of the country's political and economic dominance by the eighteenth century.

  * Such changes in the economy had a considerable impact upon the structure of society. Medieval society has been described as a feudal pyramid. It was based upon the ownership of land, military service and peasant agriculture. At the top of the pyramid was the king, who was the largest landowner. The military élites were made up of the aristocracy and their families, who held land from the king, and the knights and their families, who held land from the aristocracy. Below them came the great mass of the peasantry, who worked the land and provided food and labour for the élites. The only groups outside this structure were the clergy and the small number of people who lived in towns. The economic developments of the late Middle Ages began to change this structure, but it was a very long and gradual process.

  * Many historians agree that the most significant shift among the élites was the rise of 'the gentry', the smaller landowners below the aristocracy. Revisionist historians link this development with the expansion of the State. They consider that the gentry increased in numbers and power because of the growth in royal patronage and the opportunities to hold government office. Other historians, particularly Marxists, see the gentry rising at the expense of the aristocracy because of their greater ability and willingness to take advantage of commercial opportunities available after the fourteenth-century crisis. It is difficult to choose between these two theories. What is certain is that there were more openings by the sixteenth century than during the Middle Ages for men of initiative to increase their power and wealth.

The gentry are seen as an expanding group ranked below the aristocracy and above the yeomen. They included younger sons from the aristocracy and the upper ranks of the yeomen, as well as wealthy merchants, lawyers and professional men from the towns. Many Marxist historians see the English gentry as the rising, capitalistic bourgeoisie, which was in conflict with the aristocracy. This is a difficult argument to sustain because many gentry families were related to the aristocracy, and the ambition of successful gentry families was to join the ranks of the aristocracy. It is certainly true that the gentry, who were becoming increasingly educated through attending university and being trained in law, competed with the aristocracy for offices in central and local government. They are seen also as supplying the capitalistic drive needed to bring about economic expansion, but there is no real evidence to show that the gentry were more commercially motivated than many of the aristocracy. What can be said is that the élites in general benefited during the sixteenth century from rising prices, and the redistribution of monastic and other church lands. Only by the end of the century did the rising demand for land and titles begin to cause real competition among the élites. However, this process was only just beginning by the middle of the century, although there were already some significant developments taking place.

*Equally significant changes were taking place among the non-élites. The spread of commercialisation placed considerable pressure on the traditional village structure. The peasant way of life, where work was carried out by the family in the home and around the small holding was beginning to disappear. The enclosure of open fields and commons in some areas meant that not only were peasant smallholdings being absorbed into larger commercial farms, but that peasant families could no longer use the commons for such things as grazing their animals, collecting firewood or gathering fruit and berries. Those families who could not find work as wage labourers on the large commercial farms run by the gentry and yeomen, or in local rural industry, were forced to move away from the village. Many migrated to the towns, where they joined a growing urban proletariat dependent on wage labour. It must be stressed that changes were generally very slow, and varied widely across the country. A great many villages remained entirely unaltered. Only in the Midlands and around expanding towns, where commercial farming was profitable, were large numbers of people forced off the land. Even so, for a government anxious to maintain the status quo and the traditional village structure, this was not an ideal situation. In an attempt to stop people from moving away from the villages the government tried to legislate against enclosure, which they thought was the main cause of depopulation. To stop people moving about the countryside, laws of increasing severity were passed against vagrancy. What the government failed to realise, however, was that a rising population and the shortage of job opportunities was the real underlying cause of this problem. It was this situation, worsened by increasingly frequent food shortages, that was the major cause of popular discontent in mid-sixteenth-century England.

*Religious change is seen by many historians as being very important in this economic and social restructuring. Support for the English Reformation by a large cross-section of the more commercially motivated aristocracy and gentry is interpreted as showing hostility towards the Catholic Church. The break from Rome can be seen as the removal of the 'dead hand' of a church which, by its opposition to commerce and competition, was slowing the pace of economic development. At the same time the enormous wealth and great territorial possessions of the Roman Church in England were perceived as unproductive. It is suggested that support from the élites for Henry VIII's religious policy was based on their desire to acquire confiscated church property, which they could use commercially to their own profit. Certainly the seizure, and after 1540 the sale, of monastic lands was the largest redistribution of property since the Norman Conquest of 1066 and enabled an expansion in the numbers of the land-owning élites. However, there is little evidence to show that the Catholic élites were any less eager to acquire church property, or were less commercially successful, than their Protestant counterparts. Consequently, while it is possible to say that the Reformation promoted commercial change, it is more difficult to maintain that it was brought about for commercial reasons.

The impact of religious change on the lower orders is equally difficult to define. Many among the rural population were opposed to Protestantism, seeing it as a threat to their traditional way of life. Others, especially in the towns, welcomed the ideas of the reformers on the natural rights of man, equality, and the re-distribution of church wealth. These different responses to Protestantism are seen by many Marxist historians as evidence of the loss of solidarity among the lower orders and of the beginning of the breakdown of community values and mutual support. Protestantism is perceived as introducing more radical ideas into popular protest, or, at least, strengthening those that already existed. Although extreme radical groups among the lower orders in England were always to be a minority, they are seen as playing an important part in increasing social tensions and pressures. For them the Reformation marked the beginning of the millenium, the thousand year rule of Christ, when all men would be equal and there would be no more hardship, poverty and unemployment. Obviously such ideas were very attractive in a period of sharply rising prices, food shortages and a lack of job opportunities, and increased the possibility of popular riot and rebellion in years of particular hardship. This was clearly a dangerous situation, and fear of popular rebellion added to the stresses already being felt within society. Although many of these social, economic and religious changes were only beginning to be known in England by 1550, they can be seen as posing very serious problems to

the government and represented a potential crisis for the State.
These issues will be discussed in greater detail in Chapters 4, 5 and 6.

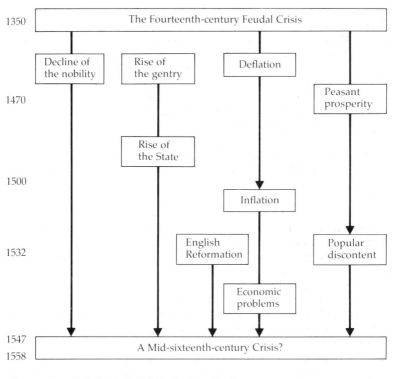

Summary – A Crisis in Mid-Tudor England?

Making notes on 'A Crisis in Mid-Tudor England?'

This chapter is designed to show you how the views of historians about mid-sixteenth-century England have changed, the difference of opinion between schools of historians, and how they use the concepts of crisis and the development of the State to interpret events. You will need this interpretive framework to help you make sense of the events discussed in the other chapters of this book. The chapter is mainly concerned with political, religious, social and economic problems, and how they might have been a cause of crisis. Your notes should identify the main problems to help you decide if they really were a cause of crisis. Make sure you show the differences between long and short-term causes. The following headings and questions should help you:

1. Introduction.
1.1. What are the two main schools of thought among historians and how do they differ?
1.2. What is meant by crisis, and what are the dangers of using general theories?
1.3. What are seen as the two main causes of crisis? How did they affect England?
2. A Crisis of the State: Politics, Religion and Foreign Policy.
2.1. How is the State seen to develop?
2.2. What part did the monarch play in the English State? What were the constitutional problems, and did they represent a crisis?
2.3. What were the main causes of quarrels among the ruling élites in England?
2.4. Why was foreign policy important to the State? What problems did England face?
3. A Crisis of the State: Social, Religious and Economic Change.
3.1. How and why did agricultural difficulties cause problems?
3.2. Why was there an urban crisis? What were the industrial changes and problems? How did they add to urban problems?
3.3. How and why did the Atlantic economy develop? Why is religion thought to have played an important part in the development of capitalism and world trade? Why did England play little part in world trade until after 1550?
3.4. What social changes and problems were caused by commercialism? Why is the rise of the gentry in England seen as being so important? How did Protestantism influence both the élites and the non-élites?

Answering essay questions on 'Edward VI and Mary: The Mid-Tudor Crisis'

Examiners have proved themselves to be very resourceful in designing questions on this period. There are, therefore, no 'stock' questions for which it is necessary to prepare. You must expect to be asked to tackle questions that group together aspects of the topic in a wide variety of ways.

These groups of aspects fall into three main categories:

a) General questions covering all aspects over the entire period.
b) Detailed questions concentrating on one aspect over the entire period.

c) Detailed questions concentrating on one or more aspects over part of the period.

Study the six questions below. Assign them to the three categories above.

1. 'Why was Mary I so unpopular?'
2. 'To what extent was there a mid-century crisis during the reigns of Edward VI and Mary I?'
3. 'Why was there such instability in England between 1547 and 1558?'
4. '"English foreign policy under Edward VI and Mary was a failure." Do you agree?'
5. 'Was the Duke of Northumberland a worse ruler than the Duke of Somerset?'
6. 'What were the problems facing the English economy in the mid-sixteenth century?'

The book has been structured so that each of Chapters 2–6 provides a discussion of a single aspect over the entire period. Which category of questions will this structure most directly help you to answer? Questions from this category will be considered at the end of Chapters 2, 3, 4 and 6. Questions from the other categories will be discussed in a separate section on page 149.

Source-based questions on 'A Crisis in Mid-Tudor England?'

1 The Nature of the State
Read the extracts from the writings of John Pym and from the Treason Act of 1547, given on pages 5 and 6. Answer the following questions:

a) Explain the meaning of (i) 'the common good' in the first extract, and (ii) 'commonwealth' in the second extract. (2 marks)
b) Both extracts describe what constitutes a well balanced State. What are the similarities and differences between the two descriptions? (8 marks)
c) What can be deduced from the extracts about the values and attitudes of the two authors? (6 marks)
d) How 'reactionary' or 'revolutionary' do the views expressed in the extracts seem to you? Explain your answer. (4 marks)

2 Edward VI and his Privy Council, 1551
Study the illustration of Edward VI and his Privy Council which is reproduced on page 7. Answer the following questions:

a) How old was Edward in 1551? (1 mark)

b) What were the probable aims of the artist in creating this picture? Comment in particular on the role of the monarchy. (7 marks)

c) How does the artist attempt to achieve his aims? Comment on the overall composition of the picture as well as referring to details within it. (8 marks)

d) How reliable is this illustration as a source of information about what happened at meetings of the Privy Council in 1551? Explain your answer. (4 marks)

CHAPTER 2

Politics and the State

1 Introduction

Political history is about a small élite of men and women who run the day-to-day affairs of a country. In trying to interpret events, political historians have to rely upon written evidence. State papers make it easy to discover what happened when. It is more difficult to find out why things happened. This is particularly true for the sixteenth century because many of the documents have been lost, or destroyed. However, lack of evidence is only part of the political historian's problem. Successful political leaders tend to create their own history. Being in power they can create evidence which sets their actions in the best possible light. On the other hand, statesmen who fail are often unjustly condemned by those who replace them. The eleven years between 1547 and 1558 saw many such shifts in political power. It is for these reasons that political historians continue to re-assess their views about mid-Tudor statesmen.

*Until some fifteen years ago historians generally accepted the interpretation that the mid-sixteenth century was a time of political conflict and confrontation in England – a period of failure and lack of progress, set between the great achievements of the 1530s and the recovery of the national economy under Elizabeth I. This was seen to stem from weak political leadership. The result was a contest between Crown and Parliament, and bitter strife between Catholics and Protestants. The three major political figures – the Dukes of Somerset and Northumberland and Queen Mary – have been blamed for this failure for various reasons. The 'good Duke' of Somerset was seen as a moderate reformer, who fell from power because of his tolerant and humanitarian policies. The Duke of Northumberland was considered ruthless and greedy, creating a constitutional crisis by trying to change the succession. Mary was condemned as inept for her obsession with Philip II of Spain and her devotion to Catholicism. The great debate between Marxist and revisionist historians in the 1960s and 1970s did little to change this picture. General theories of crisis and the rise of the State only strengthened the opinion that the mid-Tudor period was one of failure and crisis. However, new evidence and research has caused these views to be questioned and revised.

The idea of a mid-Tudor crisis is no longer popular. Considerable reservations are felt about the theories of the State and the Tudor revolution in government. The period 1547–58 is now seen in terms of of constructive debate and cooperation rather than conflict – as a time of definite political and administrative development. In part this change results from revised opinions about the political leaders. The Duke of

Somerset is now seen as a typical Tudor soldier and statesman who was more interested in war than humanitarian reform. While the Duke of Northumberland is still regarded as ruthless and self-seeking, he is becoming recognised as an able and reforming administrator. Although no-one has claimed that Mary was a great queen, her reign is being seen as a time of significant political and administrative progress.

2 The Last Years of Henry VIII

In 1540 the fall of Thomas Cromwell, Henry VIII's chief adviser in the 1530s, heralded a period of increased political instability. There was a growth in the rivalry between factions at Court. The main issue lay between the parties supporting reform in politics and religion, and those conservatives who wished to see less reform, even if not a return to Catholicism. The reform party was led by Archbishop Cranmer and Edward Seymour, later Duke of Somerset, the uncle of Prince Edward. The conservatives were headed by Thomas Howard, Duke of Norfolk, and Stephen Gardiner, Bishop of Winchester. The disgrace of Cromwell had been a success for the conservative party. It was confirmed by Henry VIII's marriage to Catherine Howard, the Duke of Norfolk's niece. However, Catherine's trial and execution for adultery in 1542 marked a victory for the reform party. For the next five years the two factions strove for supremacy at Court. Henry VIII's final marriage to Catherine Parr, a committed Protestant, showed that the conservatives were losing ground. In 1546 the reformers gained a decisive advantage when the Duke of Norfolk was arrested and put in the Tower of London on a charge of treason, and Stephen Gardiner was dismissed from the Privy Council. It was against this background that Edward VI, brought up as a Protestant, came to the throne in 1547. Some historians see these disputes between the factions as a sign of increasing dynastic weakness. Others argue that factions were a normal part of Tudor politics, and that such rivalry was necessary for healthy government.

*Apart from the wars with Scotland and France which had begun in 1542 and 1544, Henry VIII's major concern in his last years was the succession. Since 1527 he had been obsessed with the need to safeguard the dynasty by leaving a male heir to succeed him. The birth of Prince Edward in 1537 had seemed to achieve this objective. By 1546 the King's declining health made it clear that his son would come to the throne as a minor. To avoid any possible disputes Henry made a final settlement of the succession in his Will of 1546. This replaced the Succession Acts of 1534, 1536 and 1544. The terms of the Will were similar to the Act of 1544. In the event of Edward dying without heirs, the succession was to pass first to Mary, the daughter of Catherine of Aragon. If Mary died without heirs her sister Elizabeth, daughter of Ann Boleyn, was to succeed. The major addition to the previous settlement was that if all Henry's children were to die without heirs, the

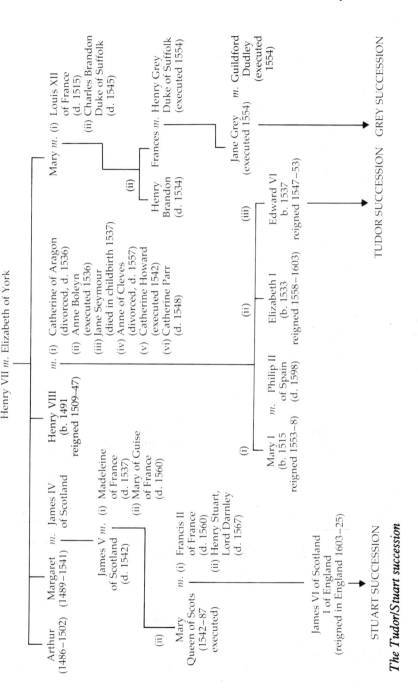

The Tudor/Stuart succession

throne was to pass to his niece Frances Grey. Lady Frances was the elder daughter of Henry VIII's sister Mary, who first had married King Louis XII of France and then Charles Brandon, Duke of Suffolk. This clause meant that the other possible claimant to the English throne, the infant Mary Queen of Scots, was excluded. Mary was the descendant of Henry VIII's sister Margaret, who had married James IV of Scotland (see page 23). Although the Will had replaced the earlier succession settlements, the Acts of 1534 and 1536, which had made Mary and Elizabeth illegitimate, were not repealed. This, and the exclusion of Mary Queen of Scots, was to cause constitutional difficulties later.

*Henry's other major concern in his Will was to try to prevent the almost inevitable power struggle which would follow his death. To achieve this he set up a Privy Council of 16 of his most trusted advisers. Aware of the tensions between the reform party and the conservatives, he tried to balance the membership of the Council between the two factions. Members of the Council were to have equal powers, and were to govern the country until Edward reached 18 years of age. Unfortunately for the success of this plan, the arrest of the Duke of Norfolk and the expulsion of Gardiner from the Privy Council had removed the leaders of the conservative party. Although Henry's death on 27 January 1547 saved the Duke of Norfolk from execution, it left the Protestant party firmly in control.

3 The Protector Somerset 1547-9

In spite of Henry's precautions it soon became apparent that the plans for the regency were not practical. Even without the tensions between the conservative and reform parties, it is doubtful whether a Regency Council made up of 16 equal members could have operated successfully. The Council system of government in England was designed to function with a chief executive, the monarch, to make final decisions. For the Regency Council to operate successfully it was necessary for one of its members to act as chief executive. Edward Seymour quickly emerged as the leader of the Council. He had been high in favour during the last part of Henry VIII's reign and this, coupled with the reputation that he had earned through his successful campaigns in the Scottish war, placed him in a very strong position. He and his ally and fellow councillor, Sir William Paget, had custody of Henry VIII's Will. They kept the King's death secret for four days. This gave them time to take advantage of the weakness of the conservative party and to rally support among the reformers and moderates for the nomination of Seymour as leader of the Council. The reason why Seymour gained power so quickly is not altogether clear, although his being the new King's uncle certainly helped. Clearly the reformers among the clergy hoped for the introduction of religious reform, and it is likely that many moderates regarded Seymour as the best means of preserving stability and the royal supremacy.

Henry's death and the terms of the Will were made known to an assembly of nobles and higher clergy at the Tower of London on 1 February. At the same time Lord Wriothesley, the Chancellor and new head of the conservative party, announced that Edward Seymour had been made leader of the Council for 'the better conduct of business'. By the end of February Seymour had secured the firm support of the majority of councillors and was made Lord Protector, with the right to appoint and dismiss members of the Privy Council. These powers made Seymour the undisputed ruler of the country. He was created Duke of Somerset and was given confiscated monastic property to support his new titles. This has been seen by some historians as a sign of his greed. However, most members of the Council were given new titles and estates, so it can be interpreted as the winners of the power struggle sharing out the spoils of victory.

* Somerset's success in reaching supreme power is often attributed to the support of the very able Paget. Therefore, any valid judgement of Somerset's character and capability has to be based on his achievements, or lack of them, over the ensuing two years. There are three main views about his character. In the past he has been regarded as a genuine humanitarian, sympathetic to the plight of the poor. More recently, doubts were expressed as to whether he had any interest in social reform and it has been claimed that he was an arrogant self-seeker who refused to accept advice, and enriched himself with confiscated church property. Using the same evidence, historians currently see him as a typical Tudor soldier and statesman, whose main interest was the war against Scotland and France. As such he is regarded as being no more greedy, and no more sympathetic to the poor, than his fellow aristocrats. Certainly in February 1547 the other members of the Council were just as quick to seize lands and titles as Somerset himself.

* Somerset took over a form of administration that had been developed by Henry VII and Henry VIII. Tudor government rested on the principle that the power of the monarch was based in Parliament. Both houses of Parliament had to approve proposals for taxation and confirm any new laws before they became permanent statutes. On the other hand the monarch could call Parliament to meet as often, or as infrequently, as he chose. When Parliament was not in session the Crown could make new laws through proclamations, or suspend existing laws, but these actions had to be confirmed when Parliament met again. Certain things such as diplomacy and the making of war or peace were part of the royal prerogative, over which the monarch had complete control. Religion had always been considered part of the royal prerogative until Henry VIII used Parliament to carry through the English Reformation. Under Mary, and later Elizabeth I, religion was

to become a matter of dispute between Crown and Parliament. The day-to-day administration was carried out by the Privy Council. Members of the Council were chosen by the monarch from among the nobles, higher clergy and more important gentry. They were selected for their loyalty and their administrative or military skills, and could be dismissed at will. The work of the Privy Council was supported by a staff of permanent civil servants chosen mainly from the gentry, lawyers and minor clergy. The Privy Council was responsible also for the running of local government, with the support of the nobles, higher clergy and gentry. The two parts of the country which were thought most open to rebellion or invasion, Wales and the Scottish border, were administered by the Councils of Wales and of the North. These were regarded as sub-committees of the Privy Council, and were run by members of the local élites chosen by the Privy Council in London. Local government in the remainder of England was administered by the nobles and higher clergy in each county. They were expected to maintain order, administer justice, collect taxes, raise troops, and carry out instructions from the Privy Council. These duties had to be organised through their own households, and frequently at their own expense. In turn they were supported by the local gentry, who, among other things, acted as Justices of the Peace and commissioners for collecting taxes and mustering the county militias. The major problem with this system was that if the leading local families did not support the government, or did not like the legislation, they refused to carry out instructions from London. This meant that the central administration had to be careful to maintain the confidence and support of the majority of the landed élites.

There is little to suggest that the administration during the first two years of Edward VI's reign was markedly different from that of the last years of Henry VIII. The Privy Council was made up of men who had risen to power under Henry VIII and who were using the same methods and machinery of government to cope with similar problems. The real difference was the lack of effective leadership, and the fact that the problems had grown worse. Economic and financial expedients and a half-hearted religious reform policy only created confusion and uncertainty among both the landed élites and the general public. It has been suggested that Somerset was neither more nor less to blame than his aristocratic colleagues. But whether this was because he was unwilling, or unable to change their attitudes is uncertain. While there is no evidence that he tried to corrupt the government, it is equally true that he introduced no reforms. What can be said is that he failed to show the leadership necessary to compensate for the absence of an adult monarch. Whether this was because of his preoccupation with the war effort, or because of his stubbornness and inability to adjust to new conditions is difficult to judge.

*Apart from three pressing short-term problems, the new regime in

Edward VI c.1546

1547 inherited a variety of long-term difficulties from the previous reign. Immediate decisions had to be made as to whether to continue the wars against Scotland and France, the question of religious reform, and how to find ways of raising more revenue. Whether or not Somerset's main interest was to bring the war to a successful conclusion, its continuation (see Chapter 3) was seen as a matter of national pride by the aristocracy and gentry. Consequently, any move to end the war would have lost him support among the landed élites. In any case the Council was bound by Henry VIII's last wishes to arrange a marriage between Edward VI and the infant Mary Queen of Scots to secure the succession.

In 1539 Henry VIII had tried to prevent any further religious changes by the Act of Six Articles, which had laid down doctrines and forms of worship for the Church of England. Since then pressure had been mounting among the Protestant clergy and laity for the introduction of reforms along the lines of Lutheranism and Calvinism on the continent. Although the Privy Council was made up mainly of moderates, it was anxious to keep the support of influential reformers such as Bishops Ridley and Latimer. For this reason the administration had to make some gesture towards introducing religious reform if it was not to risk losing the support of the Protestant activists and encourage a Catholic revival, which might well have resulted in it losing power.

Revenue was the most pressing problem. In 1547 the country was virtually bankrupt. The crippling cost of the war was the main reason for this. By 1546 Henry VIII had already spent £2,100,000 on the war, and borrowed a further £152,000 from continental bankers. To pay for this he had sold off most of the monastic lands seized between 1538 and 1540, as well as some crown lands. By 1547 the annual revenue from crown lands had fallen to £200,000. This was insufficient to run the country and pay off government borrowing, let alone finance the war. There was an urgent need to reform the taxation and customs system, and bring the financial administration up to date. Somerset and the Council, possibly because of their preoccupation with the war, did none of these things. Instead they fell back on the old expedients of seizing more church property and debasing the coinage (see page 30).

*As well as these immediate political and administrative difficulties, the government faced a number of serious long-term economic and social problems. Population continued to rise, and this presented a major threat to the government. Increasing population was the main cause of inflation because greater demand for goods pushed up prices. Not only did this add to the cost of administration, but it also threatened the living standards of the great mass of the population at a time when wages were not increasing. In addition it meant that more people were available for employment. This in turn caused more poverty because it also raised the number of vagrants looking for work. Social distress was made worse because harvest failures were becoming more frequent, making famines more likely and increasing the price of grain. As the situation grew worse, so the level of popular discontent rose (see Chapters 5 and 6). The root causes of these problems were largely beyond the government's control, but clearly the administration did not understand the problems, which meant that the solutions they tried frequently made the situation worse. On the existing evidence it is difficult to decide whether the authorities were really concerned about social and economic reform, or whether their main objective was to prevent public disorder (see page 31). Certainly the ruling élites feared popular riot and rebellion, which they regarded as a threat to the whole structure of society.

Somerset and the Privy Council, therefore, were faced with a considerable dilemma. They had to continue the war for the sake of national prestige and to retain the support of a large section of the élites. If they maintained the war effort the country would be plunged further into debt. However, if they raised taxes this would be unpopular with the élites and other taxpayers. At the same time they had to take some action over religious reform if they were not to lose the support of the Protestant activists. Such a loss of support might allow a Catholic revival and, thus, endanger their hold on power. Yet if they went too far the reformers might provoke the Catholics into open rebellion. The administration was well aware that there was rising popular discontent over the worsening economic conditions. This they feared might easily lead to popular uprisings, but they were uncertain how to tackle the economic problems. From their actions over the next two years the government's main objective appears to have been to continue the wars. At the same time it cautiously introduced some religious reforms and tried to damp down popular discontent.

*When the government had established itself in power and decided its legislative programme, Parliament was summoned to meet on 4 November 1547. One of the first actions was to pass a new Treason Act. This repealed the old heresy, treason and censorship laws and the Act of Six Articles which had maintained doctrinal orthodoxy since 1539. The removal of the heresy laws allowed people to discuss religion freely without fear of arrest, while the ending of censorship on printing and publishing enabled the circulation of books and pamphlets on religion, and the importation of Lutheran and Calvinist literature. A whole mass of unpopular legislation passed during the previous reign was thus swept away. In the past this has been seen as clear proof of Somerset's toleration. Yet it can equally well be interpreted as the normal action of a new regime trying to gain popularity by abolishing the oppressive legislation of its predecessor. However, closer examination suggests ~~But~~ that the government was clearing the way for religious reforms (see Chapter 4).

Whatever prompted the government to pass a new Treason Act, it immediately created problems for itself. The removal of the restrictive laws encouraged widespread debate over religion (see page 71), particularly in London and other towns. Public meetings frequently ended in disorder and riots, with attacks on churches to break up statues of saints and other Catholic images. At the same time the repeal of the old laws left the county and urban authorities with much less power to deal with such situations. Consequently the government had helped to promote the very disorder that it was trying to avoid. At the same time it had undermined the confidence of the élites, who felt themselves powerless to enforce order.

*The new Treason Act also repealed the Proclamation Act of 1539, by which royal proclamations had to be obeyed as if they were acts of Parliament, providing that they did not infringe existing laws. Although Tudor monarchs had, and would continue to use proclamations (see page 32), the Proclamation Act had been regarded with suspicion because it was feared that it would allow the monarch to rule without Parliament. However, the repeal of the Act did not mean that proclamations could not be used. Indeed, because the limitations previously imposed by the 1539 Act had been removed, it has been suggested that Somerset was trying to give himself more freedom to rule without Parliament. There is no evidence to suggest that this was Somerset's real intention, but there was a considerable increase in the use of proclamations during his period of office. Under Henry VIII proclamations were, on average, used six times a year. During Edward VI's reign they averaged 19 per year, and of these, 77 – well over half – were issued by Somerset. This increase is now seen as a strategy adopted by a government, faced with severe difficulties, which needed to react as quickly as possible to changing circumstances. Certainly contemporaries did not seem to think that Somerset was trying to corrupt the constitution. There is no evidence that he did not have the backing of the Privy Council, and there is no sign of protest from Parliament about their use.

*The Chantries Act of 1547 might be seen as another measure of religious reform. Undoubtedly it was a logical step after the dissolution of the monasteries to close the chantries, which were small religious houses endowed with lands to support a priest whose duty it was to sing masses for the soul of the founder. Yet, in reality, this Act was a device to raise money to pay for the wars. A similar plan had already been discussed by Henry VIII and his advisers. Commissioners were sent out early in 1548 to visit the chantries, confiscate their land and property, and collect all the gold and silver plate attached to them. The latter was then melted down to make coins. Simultaneously the royal mints were ordered to re-issue the coinage and reduce the silver content by adding copper. The coinage had already been debased in 1543 and there were to be further debasements until 1551, by which time the silver content had been reduced to 25 per cent. Although these measures provided much needed revenue, they created further problems. By increasing the number of coins in circulation the government was adding to inflation. Prices, particularly for grain, rose rapidly, fuelling discontent among the poor.

*That the maintenance of public order was very much in the mind of the administration is shown by the Vagrancy Act of 1547. The harshness of this legislation shows little concern for the poor and needy. The earlier poor law of 1536 did recognise that the able-bodied were having difficulty in finding work, and ordered parishes to support the impotent poor. The 1547 Act was a savage attack on vagrants looking for work, who were seen by the government as a cause of riots and sedition. Under the new law any able-bodied person out of work for more than three days was to be branded with a V and sold into slavery for two years. Further offences were to be punished with permanent slavery. The children of vagrants could be taken from their parents and set to work as apprentices in useful occupations. The new law was widely unpopular, and many of the county and urban authorities refused to enforce it. Although it also proposed housing and collections for the disabled, this measure does little to support Somerset's reputation for humanitarianism.

*By the middle of 1548 it is clear that popular discontent was rising because the Privy Council was forced to take measures to appease public agitation. It has been suggested that this legislation formed part of a reform programme put forward by John Hales at the Treasury and the so-called 'commonwealth men', supported by Somerset. In the light of the evidence this interpretation is now regarded as being very suspect, and there are increasing doubts as to whether such a group ever existed. It seems more likely that growing discontent over rising prices and food shortages, following harvest failures, forced the government to take some piecemeal action. Here again Somerset's reputation as a reformer and a friend to the people is very much open to question. The trouble was that the government blamed all the economic problems on enclosure. It was felt that the fencing-off of common land for sheep pasture and the consequent eviction of peasant families from their homes was the major cause of inflation and unemployment. Proclamations were issued against enclosures, and commissioners were sent out to investigate abuses. The main effect of these measures was to increase unrest. Hopes were raised among the masses that the government would take some decisive action, which it did not. Fear grew among the landed élites that the authorities would actually prevent this form of estate improvement. Further measures limiting the size of leaseholds and placing a tax on wool only made the situation worse by increasing these fears. In any case many of the élites evaded the legislation, which, consequently, fell most heavily on the poorer sections of society it was supposed to protect.

The government seemed to be more concerned with avoiding riot and rebellion than with helping the poor and solving economic problems.

This suspicion is supported by three proclamations issued in 1548 aimed specifically at maintaining law and order. A ban on football was rigorously enforced on the grounds that games usually ended in riots and disorder. It also became an offence to spread rumours, as they were likely to create unrest. Finally, all unlawful assemblies were forbidden. Anyone found guilty of these offences was to be sent for varying periods to the galleys – royal warships propelled by oars. These seem like emergency measures passed by a government which realised that the economic position was getting out of hand, and feared the consequences.

It appears that these efforts had little effect and in 1549 the country drifted into a major crisis. Somerset seemed unable, or unwilling, to take decisive action to suppress peasant uprisings in the West Country and East Anglia (see Chapters 4 and 6). Traditionally his unwillingness to act has been interpreted as showing sympathy. However, it seems more likely that the initial delays were caused by the reluctance of the local élites to intervene without government support. Lack of money made it difficult to raise a new mercenary army, and Somerset, as Commander-in-Chief, was reluctant to withdraw troops from his garrisons in Scotland and France. It was only when the Privy Council realised the seriousness of the situation and provided enough troops that Lord Russell in the West Country and John Dudley, Earl of Warwick, in East Anglia were able to defeat the rebels. A major consequence of the rebellions was the fall of Somerset, whose colleagues quickly abandoned him as a man who had failed to prevent anarchy and revolution. When his chief rival, John Dudley, fresh from his victory in Norfolk, engineered Somerset's arrest in October 1549 there was no opposition. Although Somerset was released early the following year and rejoined the Privy Council, within a year he was accused of plotting against the government. He was executed in January 1552.

4 The Lord President Northumberland 1550–3

Even before his arrest on 11 October 1549, it was clear that Somerset was discredited and had lost control of the political situation. Many members of the Privy Council were offended by his aloofness and his arrogance in using his own household instead of the Council to conduct business. He had undermined the confidence of the aristocracy and the gentry because of his inept handling of the peasant uprisings, while his religious reforms (see Chapter 4) had alienated even moderates among the conservative party. A power struggle soon developed in which John Dudley was a leading contender. Dudley crushed the rebel army in Norfolk on 26 August and returned to London on 14 September. This gave him a distinct advantage because as the commander of the main army in England he controlled the capital. Almost immediately he began to negotiate with Lords Arundel and Wriothesley, leaders of the conservative party. In desperation, on 30 September, Somerset issued a proclamation ordering all troops in England to return to their duties in Scotland and France. On 5 October he issued another proclamation for a general array of loyal troops for the defence of the realm. There was no response, and Somerset removed the Royal Household from Hampton Court to Windsor Castle for security. Meanwhile the Privy Council protected its own position by issuing a proclamation blaming Somerset for the rebellions. All parties were anxious to avoid civil war. On 8 October Somerset agreed to negotiate on honourable terms, and was arrested three days later.

 *John Dudley, like Somerset, had risen to political prominence during the last years of Henry VIII's reign. He, too, had gained a good military reputation in the Scottish and French wars. He was a member of the Council named in Henry's Will and was ambitious for more power. The events of 1549 gave him his opportunity to take advantage of Somerset's political isolation. By mid-September he had emerged as the major rival for power, and contrived to have Somerset arrested. At this point Dudley showed his considerable ability as a politician. By pretending to be a Catholic sympathiser, he successfully conspired with the conservatives. This gave him control of the Council. However, the conservatives were secretly planning to seize power and have Dudley arrested along with Somerset. Simultaneously Dudley was plotting with the reform party, particularly Archbishop Cranmer, who had considerable influence in the Royal Household. With Cranmer's help he gained control over the administration of the Royal Household, which gave him immediate access to Edward VI. This enabled him to gain the confidence of the King, and by February 1550 he was in a strong enough position to have the conservatives expelled from the Council. To secure his position he became Lord President of the Council. In April he was made General Warden of the North, which gave him military command. However, he only achieved complete power in October 1551 when he had Somerset re-arrested, and was made Duke of Northumberland. In spite of his continuing reputation for greed and ruthlessness, historians are beginning to recognise Northumberland as an ambitious, but able, politician. In marked contrast to Somerset he introduced a series of significant and lasting reforms.

 Northumberland had learned from Somerset's mistakes, and saw that control of the Council was the key to political power. As Lord President he was able to appoint and dismiss councillors at will, and had complete control over procedure. Able supporters of Somerset, like Paget and William Cecil, who had been arrested, were released and allowed to return to their posts. To increase his authority Northumberland enlarged the membership of the Council to 33, selecting councillors upon whose loyalty he could rely. Whenever possible he chose men of military experience, so that in the event of further rebellions, he, unlike Somerset, could be sure of immediate armed support. To make the Council more efficient and stable Northumberland created a smaller, inner committee with a fixed routine to conduct business. Learning from Somerset's mistake in frequently by-passing the Privy Council, Northumberland restored it to the centre of government. For similar reasons he made less use of proclamations, preferring to use Parliament to confirm legislation whenever possible.

   *The political difficulties facing the new government were the same as those which Somerset had failed to resolve. Unfortunately for Northumberland they had become more acute. The most pressing problems were the diplomatic position and revenue. The war situation had deteriorated because the French, taking advantage of England's domestic problems, had declared open warfare in August 1549. This placed Boulogne (see Chapter 3) under serious threat. Although the élites were eager to continue hostilities, Northumberland, very sensibly in contrast to Somerset, realised that England was in an impossible military and financial position. He ended the war with France and withdrew many of the garrisons from Scotland. However, while this eased the immediate difficulties, diplomatic relations with Charles V became strained as the Emperor mistrusted England's new position of neutrality towards France. At the same time Northumberland was still in the process of gaining supreme power. To achieve this end he allied himself with the more extreme Protestant reformers, such as Bishops Ridley and Hooper. In return for their political support Northumberland had to allow the Church of England to swing towards Calvinism (see page 78). This still further antagonised Charles V, who favoured moderation in the English Church, and England became diplomatically isolated.

   *Revenue remained a serious problem; England was bankrupt in 1549. Somerset had spent £1,356,000 on the war, and sold crown lands to the value of £800,000. The government even had to borrow to raise the £50,000 a year needed to maintain the Royal Household. Ending the war drastically reduced expenditure, but a number of expedients had to be adopted to keep the government solvent. In May 1551 the coinage was debased for the last time. Although inflation rose still further the government made a profit of £114,000 to pay immediate expenses and short-term loans. Even so, a further £243,000 had to be borrowed from continental bankers. William Cecil, restored as Secretary of State, was put in charge of financial planning. He was assisted by Sir Thomas Gresham from the Treasury. They recommended the sale of chantry lands and church plate to start paying off loans. The London trading companies agreed to support government debts and more money was raised from the mints and crown lands. Gresham was sent to the Netherlands with £12,000 a week to manipulate the stock market, restore the value of sterling against continental currencies and pay off loans. In March 1552 the coinage was called in and re-issued with the silver content restored to that of 1527. This helped to slow the rise in inflation and restore confidence in sterling. Strict economies were made in government spending, and Northumberland paid off the remainder of his mercenary troops. By these means most of the overseas debts were liquidated and a 'privy coffer', a contingency fund, was established. By 1553 the financial situation had been stabilised. Even so, another £140,000 worth of crown lands had to be sold to replace the revenue taxes, voted unwillingly by Parliament, which were not collected because they were so unpopular. However, Northumberland had shown considerable political coolness and skill in resolving a serious financial crisis. Unlike Somerset, he had displayed the ability to delegate authority, and skill in selecting the right people for the task.

At the same time there was a concerted effort to improve the efficiency of the financial machinery. The most pressing need was to streamline the collection of royal revenue and to find ways of increasing government income. In 1552 a commission began to investigate the five revenue courts which carried out the work of the Exchequer. The report recommended that to avoid corruption and inefficiency the number of courts should be reduced to two – the Exchequer and the Office of Crown Lands. Alternatively all the courts should be merged into the Exchequer. It was also suggested that custom and excise rates should be revised. Although these constructive proposals had to be postponed because of Edward VI's death, they were introduced in the reign of Mary.

*The government was faced by equally pressing economic and social problems. Here again the Northumberland administration showed a much more positive approach than that adopted by Somerset. Population, and with it inflation, was still rising. This meant that the living standards of the masses continued to decline, and that work was more difficult to find. In 1550 the Antwerp cloth market finally collapsed, causing widespread unemployment among textile workers in East Anglia and the West Country. The debasement of the coinage in 1551 raised inflation still further. Grain prices rose rapidly; a situation worsened by a series of harvest failures. At the beginning of 1550 the country was still simmering after the recent peasant uprisings and unsettled by the political power struggle among the privy councillors. Consequently the administration had to act carefully and skilfully if further serious disorder was to be avoided.

The 1549 rebellions had badly frightened the government, aristocracy and gentry, who drew closer together to avoid further disorder among the masses. The unpopular 1547 Vagrancy Act and the sheep tax of 1548 were repealed in 1550, and this helped to dispel unrest. In the same year a new Treason Act was passed, which restored censorship and gave the authorities more power to enforce law and order. Initially these measures helped to prevent the widespread popular discontent from turning into actual revolt. At the same time the administration tried to improve the economic situation and relieve poverty and

distress. The existing anti-enclosure legislation was rigorously enforced, and the unpopular enclosure commissions were withdrawn.
The re-evaluation of the coinage in 1552 halted inflation and reduced
prices. In the same year acts were passed to protect arable farming, and
to stop the charging of excessive interest on debts. A new poor law was
passed. Although it did nothing to help the able-bodied find work, it
did make it easier for the parish and town authorities to support the
aged, infirm and crippled. While Northumberland did little to resolve
the underlying economic problems, he did check inflation, and ease
some of the worst of the social distress.

 *By 1552 Northumberland seemed to be firmly in control. Even the
rapid swing towards Calvinism in the Church of England (see page 78)
did not appear to be provoking any serious opposition. His power,
however, depended upon the support of Edward VI. By the end of the
year the King's health was obviously deteriorating quickly, and the
problem of the succession became a central issue once again. In
accordance with Henry VIII's will, Mary was to succeed if Edward died
childless. Mary's strong Catholic sympathies made her unpopular with
the reform party and with Edward himself. To prevent a return to
Catholicism, and to retain power, Northumberland, with the full

---

*Edward VI: Letters Patent for the Limitation of the Crown 21
June 1553*

1 And forasmuch as the said limitation of the imperial crown of
  this realm, being limited by the authority of Parliament as is
  aforesaid to the said Lady Mary and Lady Elizabeth, being
  illegitimate and not lawfully begotten, forasmuch as the mar-
5 riage between our said late father and the Lady Catherine . . .
  and the Lady Anne, was clearly and lawfully undone . . . which
  said several divorcements have been severally ratified and
  confirmed by authority of divers acts of Parliament remaining
  in their full force . . . Whereby as well the said Lady Mary as
10 also the said Lady Elizabeth to all intent and purposes are and
  be clearly disabled to ask, claim, or challenge for the said
  imperial crown . . . that if the said Lady Mary or Lady
  Elizabeth should hereafter have and enjoy the said imperial
  crown of this realm, and should happen to marry with any
15 stranger born out of this realm, that then the same would
  rather adhere and practice to have the laws and customs of his
  or their own native country or countries to be practised or put
  to use within this realm . . . which would tend to the utter
  subversion of the commonwealth of this our realm . . . We
20 therefore declare [the order of succession] to be (1) sons of
  Lady Frances, if born in our lifetime, and their heirs male; (2)
  Lady Jane and her heirs male.

Mary I, 1544

support of the King, planned to change the succession. As the Succession Acts of 1534 and 1536 making Mary and Elizabeth illegitimate had not been repealed, it was decided to disinherit them in favour of the Suffolk branch of the family. Moreover Frances, Duchess of Suffolk, was passed over because she was unlikely to have male heirs and her eldest daughter, Lady Jane Grey, was chosen to succeed. To secure his own position Northumberland married his eldest son, Guildford Dudley, to Jane in May 1553.

*Unfortunately for Northumberland, Edward VI died in July before the plans for the seizure of power could be completed. Jane Grey was proclaimed Queen by Northumberland and the Council in London, while Mary proclaimed herself Queen at Framlingham Castle in Suffolk. Northumberland's mistake was to underestimate the amount of support for Mary in the country. On 14 July he marched into Suffolk with an army of 2,000 men, but his troops deserted him. The Privy Council in London hastily changed sides and proclaimed Mary as Queen. Northumberland was arrested in Cambridge, tried, and was executed on 22 August in spite of his renouncement of Protestantism. The ease with which Mary upheld her right to the throne shows the growing stability of the State and the nation. Potential political crisis had been avoided because the majority of the nation supported the rule of law and rightful succession. The direct line of descent was still considered legitimate in spite of Parliamentary Acts to the contrary. A period of dynastic weakness and minority rule had passed without the country dissolving into civil war.

Two Acts were passed, one in 1553 and another in 1554, to resolve the constitutional position. This legislation was designed to confirm Mary Tudor's legitimacy, and to establish the right of female monarchs to rule in England. However, no attempt was made to make Elizabeth legitimate, although she was recognised as Mary's heir in the event of her dying childless.

An Act Declaring Mary I Legitimate, 1553

1 ... in any other act or acts of Parliament, as whereby your Highness is named or declared to be illegitimate, or the said marriage between the said King your father and the said Queen your mother is declared to be against the word of God or by
5 any means unlawful, shall be repealed, and void and of no force nor effect, to all intents, constructions, and purposes, as if the same sentence or acts of Parliament had never been made ...

An Act concerning the Regal Power, 1554

For the avoiding and clear extinguishment of which said error
10 or doubt, [that female monarchs could not reign in England] and for a plain declaration of the laws of this realm in that behalf; be it declared and enacted by the authority of this present Parliament, that the law of this realm is and ever hath been and ought to be understood, that the kingly or regal office
15 of the realm, and all dignities, prerogative, royal power, pre-eminences, privileges, authorities, and jurisdictions thereunto annexed, united, or belonging, being invested either in male or female, are and be and ought to be taken in the one as the other ...

5 Mary Tudor 1553–8

Mary, the daughter of Catherine of Aragon, was 37 years of age when she came to the throne. During Edward VI's reign she had resisted Protestant reform just as strongly as she had under her father. While Somerset was in power she had been allowed to follow her Catholic religion in private, and she had remained on good terms with the Protector and Edward. With the swing towards Calvinism under Northumberland, increasing pressure had been put on Mary to abandon Catholicism and to conform to the doctrines of the Church of England. During this difficult period she had received constant support and advice from her Habsburg cousin, Emperor Charles V. It was fear of the Habsburgs that had prevented the reformers taking extreme measures against her. Mary was a proud woman, who resented the pressures put on her and was embittered by the treatment of her mother. This made her mistrust her English councillors when she became Queen, and lean heavily on advice from the imperial ambassador, Simon Renard.

★When Mary proclaimed herself Queen on 11 July, even Renard and Charles V had thought it a futile gesture. Yet when she entered London at the end of the month she was greeted with enormous enthusiasm. Political prisoners such as the Duke of Norfolk and Stephen Gardiner were released. Following the advice of Charles V, she showed leniency towards her opponents. Only Northumberland and two of his closest confederates were executed. Although some members of Northumberland's Council, like Cecil, were imprisoned, others, such as Paget, were allowed to join the new Privy Council. However, this auspicious opening to the reign was not to last. Mary's popularity steadily declined over the next five years. The underlying cause for this was Mary's own character. Lacking in political ability, she was very stubborn and was determined to have her own way. As a devout Catholic she was insistent that England should return to the Church of Rome. At the same time she was convinced that national safety depended on a close alliance with the Habsburgs. Her policy rested on the achievement of these two aims, but it was the implementation of these policies that was to lose her the support of the majority of people.

★The system of central and local government remained fundamentally unchanged during Mary's reign. The Privy Council continued to be the centre of the administration. One of the main criticisms of Mary's Privy Council has been that it was too large to conduct business effectively. Certainly at times the membership did reach 43. In addition it has been claimed that the Council contained too many members who had no real political ability and who lacked administrative experience. The reason for this was that in the first few weeks of her reign Mary was forced to choose councillors from her own household, and from among leading Catholic noblemen who had supported her. By October several moderate members of Northumberland's Council had been sworn in as councillors, although they were never fully in the Queen's confidence. However, they supplied a nucleus of political ability and administrative experience previously lacking. Apart from this making the Council too large, it has been suggested that it caused strong rivalry between the Catholics, led by the Chancellor, Gardiner, and the moderates, led by Paget. However, it is now thought that, although there was disagreement, these two very able politicians cooperated closely to restore effective government. In any case in March 1554, once the scare of the Wyatt rebellion had passed (see page 41), the size of the Council was modified by having a smaller central committee of the ablest politicians to transact business. Much of the original criticism of the Privy Council came from Renard, who was jealous of the Queen's English advisers and wished to maintain his own influence with Mary. The main problem was that Mary did not exert any leadership, or show any real confidence in her Council. Frequently she did not consult the Privy Council until she had already decided matters of policy in consultation with Renard.

Previously it has been maintained that Parliament was strongly opposed to Mary's policies. This view has been modified by recent research. There seems to be little evidence that Mary controlled the House of Commons by packing it with Catholic supporters through rigged elections, and she had strong support from the higher clergy in the House of Lords, especially after the imprisonment and execution of Cranmer, Ridley and Latimer. Apart from the dislike of the Spanish marriage, both Houses seem to have cooperated with the administration throughout Mary's reign. As was the case in the Privy Council, there were lively debates and criticism of policy, but these were generally constructive. Like previous Parliaments, the main interest of the members centred on local affairs and the protection of property rights.

*Mary's political inexperience and stubbornness is shown in the first major issue of the reign – the royal marriage. The Privy Council was divided on the matter. There were two possible candidates, Edward Courtenay, Earl of Devon, who was favoured by Gardiner, and Philip of Spain, who was supported by Paget. Courtenay was a descendant of the Plantagenet kings and such a marriage would have strengthened the Tudor dynasty, but Mary favoured a closer link with the Habsburgs through Philip. It was not until 27 October that Mary raised the matter in Council, and then only to announce that she was going to marry Philip. This disconcerted Gardiner, who was blamed by Mary for the petition from the House of Commons in November, asking her to marry within the realm. Mary disregarded all opposition to her plans. On 7 December a marriage treaty, drafted by Mary, Paget, Gardiner and Renard, was presented to the Council, and ratified at the beginning of January 1554. Mary had achieved her objective of forming a closer alliance with the Habsburgs. The terms of the treaty were very favourable to England. Philip was to have no regal power in England, no foreign appointments were to be made to the Privy Council, and England was not to be involved in, or pay towards the cost of any of Philip's wars. If the marriage was childless, the succession was to pass to Elizabeth. In spite of these safeguards Mary's popularity began to ebb, as many people still thought that England would be drawn into Philip's wars and become a mere province of the Habsburg Empire.

By the end of January 1554, anti-Spanish feelings led to rebellion. Unlike the uprisings in 1549 this was a political conspiracy among the élites, and there was little support from the common people. The rebellion was led by Sir James Croft, Sir Peter Carew and Sir Thomas Wyatt. These men had all held important offices at Court under both Henry VIII and Edward VI. Although they had supported Mary's accession, they feared that the growing Spanish influence would endanger their own careers. The conspirators planned to marry Elizabeth to Edward Courtenay, whom Mary had rejected. Simultaneous rebellions in the West Country, the Midlands and Kent, were to be supported by the French fleet blockading the English Channel. The plan failed because the inept Courtenay disclosed the scheme to his patron, Gardiner, before the conspirators were ready to act. In any case, Carew, Croft and the Duke of Suffolk bungled the uprisings in the West Country and the Midlands. Wyatt succeeded in raising an army in Kent, and this caused real fear in the government because the rebels were so close to the capital. The situation was made worse because the troops sent under the Duke of Norfolk to Kent deserted to the rebels. Realising the danger, the Privy Council quickly raised forces to protect London. By delaying his advance too long, Wyatt allowed the government time to organise its troops and the rebels were trapped and defeated at Ludgate. The administration had had a bad scare, and Paget suggested leniency for the rebels for fear of provoking further revolts. Apart from Wyatt and the Duke of Suffolk, only Jane Grey and Guildford Dudley were executed. After a short imprisonment Elizabeth and Courtenay were released, and Elizabeth remained next in line to the throne. Even so, anti-Spanish feelings remained high. Philip's proposed coronation was postponed, and he only remained in England for a few months before returning to Spain.

* Once the rebellion was defeated, the restoration of Catholicism (see page 81) became a political issue. Gardiner had lost Mary's favour over the Spanish marriage. In an attempt to regain it he pressed for the introduction of religious reform. He was opposed in the Council by Paget, who feared that such a policy would cause further unrest. Paget raised the matter in Parliament to try to block Gardiner's proposals. This introduced a very significant constitutional issue. Mary thought that religion was still part of the royal prerogative (see page 82). However, she was forced to concede that doctrinal changes could only be made through Parliament. In fact there was only minor opposition in

the House of Commons to the restoration of Catholicism, and this was mainly caused by fears over property rights. Such worries were removed by guarantees that there would be no attempt to take back monastic and chantry lands already sold by the Crown. By 1555 all Henrician and Edwardian religious legislation had been repealed. There was comparatively little opposition to the actual religious changes. However, many historians consider that the policy of Mary and Archbishop Pole of persecuting and burning heretics began to turn even moderate opinion against her.

*The Marian administration was still faced by the financial problems that Northumberland had been trying to resolve. Mary had been forced to give away more crown lands to re-establish some monastic foundations. Consequently it was important to increase, and to find new sources of, government income. To achieve this the Privy Council largely adopted the proposals put forward by the commissions in 1552. In 1554 drastic changes were made to the revenue courts. The Exchequer was restored as the main financial department. It took over the work of the Court of First Fruits and Tenths, which had dealt with clerical taxation, and the Court of Augmentations, which had administered income from monastic and chantry lands. The Court of Wards, which collected feudal taxation, and the Duchy of Lancaster, administering lands belonging to the monarch as Duke of Lancaster, retained their independence. It was planned to remove the large number of debased coins in circulation and to restore the full silver content of the coinage, but Mary's death meant that the scheme was not put into effect until 1560. The 1552 proposal to revise the custom rates, which had remained unchanged since 1507, was implemented. In 1558 a new Book of Rates was issued, which increased custom revenue from £29,000 to £85,000 a year. In 1555 a full survey of all crown lands was carried out. As a result rents and entry fines, a payment made by new tenants before they could take over the property, were raised in 1557. Mary died before these measures had any real effect, and it was Elizabeth I who benefited from the increased revenue from these reforms.

*During Mary's reign the general economic situation grew even worse, with a series of very bad harvests and outbreaks of epidemics. Towns were particularly badly hit, with high mortality rates and severe food shortages. The government's reaction was to continue the policy, started under Henry VIII, of restricting the movement of textile and other industries from the towns to the countryside. This, it was hoped, would prevent an increase in urban unemployment and reduce the number of vagrants seeking work. This, however, was short-sighted because what was really needed was an increase in the amount and variety of industries in both town and country, which would provide jobs for the growing number of unemployed. To achieve this the government needed to encourage the search for new overseas markets

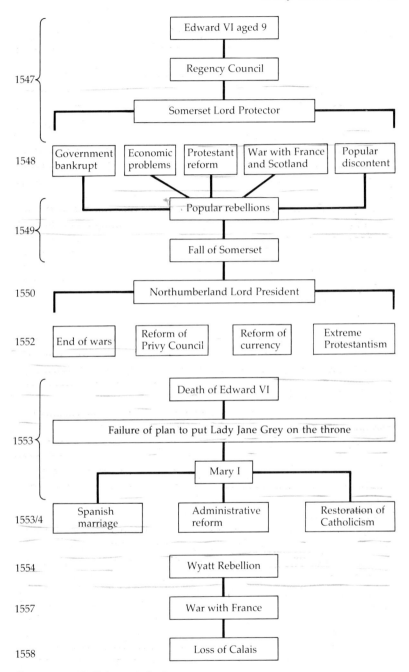

1547

Edward VI aged 9

Regency Council

Somerset Lord Protector

1548

| Government bankrupt | Economic problems | Protestant reform | War with France and Scotland | Popular discontent |

Popular rebellions

1549

Fall of Somerset

1550

Northumberland Lord President

1552

| End of wars | Reform of Privy Council | Reform of currency | Extreme Protestantism |

1553

Death of Edward VI

Failure of plan to put Lady Jane Grey on the throne

Mary I

1553/4

| Spanish marriage | Administrative reform | Restoration of Catholicism |

1554

Wyatt Rebellion

1557

War with France

1558

Loss of Calais

Summary – Politics and the State

to replace the trade lost with the collapse of the Antwerp market. In 1551 English ships had begun to trade along the north African coast, and between 1553 and 1554 Sir Hugh Willoughby was trying to find a north-east passage to the Far East (see page 58). However, until after 1558 successive English governments were too anxious to avoid offending Spain and Portugal to encourage overseas enterprise. It was not until the reign of Elizabeth I that any real progress was made in this direction.

*In spite of the assurance that England would not be involved in Spain's wars, Mary's attachment to Philip made it likely that England would be drawn into the continental conflict. As early as 1555 the Privy Council was reviewing the condition of the navy, which had been allowed to decline after Northumberland had made peace with France. A new building programme was started, improvements were made to the dockyards, and naval expenditure was increased through a new system of financing. Equal attention was paid to the army, especially after the outbreak of war in 1557. Arrangements for raising and maintaining the county militias were revised in the Militia and Arms Acts, which also improved the procedures for supplying arms and equipment. These reforms brought long-term improvements to England's military organisation.

*Philip II's visit to England early in 1557, and his success in drawing the country into his war against France, marked the final stage in Mary's growing unpopularity. The last two years of her reign saw rising anti-Spanish feelings, mounting opposition to religious persecution, and discontent with the adverse economic conditions. The war with France and the loss of Calais, England's last continental possession, united the country against the ailing Queen. The enthusiasm which marked her death in November 1558 and the succession of Elizabeth to the throne was even greater than that which had greeted Mary's overthrow of Northumberland five years earlier. Yet, despite all her failings and misguided policies, her reign was not one of complete sterility. Important reforms had been made and constitutional monarchy and the State machinery remained intact. Although the loss of Calais was seen as a national disaster, it can be interpreted as the crucial moment when England turned its attention away from fruitless continental conquest towards opportunities in the New World. Indeed, some historians would go so far as to claim that Mary's failure was her childlessness and her relatively early death, rather than her policies.

Making notes on 'Politics and the State'

This chapter is designed to show how the governments of Somerset, Northumberland and Mary dealt with long and short-term political problems. A critical issue was the succession, and you will need to take careful notes on why it was a problem and how attitudes towards the succession changed. Other key issues were war, religion and finance in both the long and short term. Economic and social questions furnished important long-term problems, causing short-term crises. You will have to decide how effective the governments were in dealing with these issues. Recently historians have revised their opinions about this period. Your notes should help you to reach conclusions about the political leaders.

The following headings, sub-headings and questions should help you:

1.   Introduction.
1.1. Why is it difficult for historians to interpret political history and judge the achievements of political leaders?
1.2. In what way did historians interpret the period until recently? How has the interpretation changed in the last 15 years?
2.   The Last Years of Henry VIII.
2.1. What was the conflict between the reform and conservative parties and how had it progressed by 1547?
2.2. Explain how Henry VIII settled the succession in 1547.
2.3. How did Henry try to prevent a power struggle after his death?
3.   The Protector Somerset 1547–9.
3.1. By what means did Somerset gain control of the Council?
3.2. How have historians' views about Somerset changed?
3.3. What was the machinery of Tudor government, and how did it operate? Why was it inefficient under Somerset?
3.4. Why were the wars and religious reform major political issues? How did Somerset try to resolve his financial problems?
3.5. What were the underlying economic and social problems? What major problems did they cause the government?
3.6. What were the government's real motives in passing the Treason Act of 1547? Why was the use of proclamations controversial?
3.7. What was the real purpose behind the passing of the Chantries Act? What were the effects of debasing the coinage?
3.8. Why was the Vagrancy Act passed in 1547? What does it tell you about Somerset? What measures were taken to prevent popular discontent and disorder? How successful were they?
3.9. Why did Somerset fall from power?
4.   The Lord President Northumberland 1550–3.
4.1. How did Somerset lose control of the political situation in 1549?
4.2. How did Northumberland take advantage of this situation to seize power?
4.3. What measures did Northumberland take to make government more efficient and so secure his own position?
4.4. In what ways did Northumberland deal with the problems of the war and religious reform?

4.5. How successful was Northumberland in coping with the financial crisis and in improving the financial administration?

4.6. In what ways were economic and social problems becoming more acute? How successful was Northumberland in solving them?

4.7. What was the succession crisis in 1553? How, and with what success, did Northumberland resolve it?

4.8. Why did Northumberland fall from power?

5. Mary Tudor 1553–8.

5.1. Why did Mary distrust her English advisers, and depend on the Habsburgs?

5.2. What two issues undermined Mary's early popularity?

5.3. How did the government operate under Mary? What, if any, were the problems with the Privy Council and Parliament?

5.4. Why was the Spanish marriage so controversial? Why did it cause rebellion?

5.5. What was Mary's religious policy, and why did it make her unpopular?

5.6. How successful and original was Mary in solving financial problems?

5.7. How did the economic and social situation grow worse?

5.8. What good results came from England's involvement in Philip II's wars?

5.9. Why was Mary so unpopular when she died?

Answering essay questions on 'Politics and the State'

Study the following questions:

1. 'Why was there political instability in England between 1547 and 1558?'

2. 'Compare and contrast the techniques of government employed by the Dukes of Somerset and Northumberland.'

3. 'To what extent was there continuity of government during the reigns of Edward VI and Mary I?'

4. '"The danger of a crisis in government between 1547 and 1558 has been greatly exaggerated." Discuss.'

Which question would best be answered by a two-part, 'to this extent yes, to this extent no' answer? Which question requires a plan made up of a number of 'because' points?

Question 2 can also be answered by a two-part approach. In this case the parts would be 'similarities' and 'differences'. Draw up a plan for this essay. Would you begin with 'similarities' or 'differences'? Why? Either approach is acceptable as long as you have a clear reason for adopting it. Where might it be appropriate to explain this reason?

Source-based questions on 'Politics and the State'

1 The Succession
Read the extracts from the Letters Patent of 21 June 1553 on page 36, the Act Declaring Mary Legitimate (1553) on page 38 and the Act concerning Regal Power (1554) on page 38. Answer the following questions:
a) Who are (i) 'our said late father' and (ii) 'Lady Frances' in the first extract, and (iii) 'the said Queen your mother' in the second extract? (3 marks)
b) Why are the words 'that female monarchs could not reign in England' in the third extract placed inside brackets? (1 mark)
c) What two arguments are used in the first extract against Mary and Elizabeth being allowed to succeed to the throne? (4 marks)
d) Which of these arguments is destroyed in the second extract? How is this done? (2 marks)
e) Why was it thought necessary to pass the Act of which the third extract is a part? (4 marks)
f) How valid is it to describe the Letters Patent of 21 June 1553 as revealing 'naked ambition without even a cloak of logical consistency to mask it'? (6 marks)

2 Edward VI and Mary
Examine the portraits of Edward VI and Mary reproduced on pages 27 and 37. Answer the following questions:
a) Both portraits were drawn before their subjects succeeded to the throne. What evidence is there in the portraits alone that this was so? (Think of several answers, including mention of what was missing.) (6 marks)
b) What reasoning would support the verdict that these portraits are 'as realistic representations as are likely to exist' of their subjects? (6 marks)
c) What are the dangers of attempting to assess personality from painted or drawn portraits? In what ways should historians use such portraits as evidence? (8 marks)

CHAPTER 3

Foreign Policy 1547–58

1 Introduction

English foreign policy between 1547 and 1558 was unsuccessful, and the country's diplomatic position was very fragile. However, it is difficult to maintain that this amounted to an actual crisis, because England was never in any real danger of foreign invasion or conquest. A major cause of England's insecurity during this period is seen to have been indecisive leadership and governmental weakness. Yet although Somerset, Northumberland and Mary can be seen to have failed to show any diplomatic leadership, they were faced with situations not of their own making, and with circumstances largely beyond their control.

In 1547 Somerset inherited Henry VIII's ambitious policy of conquest in France, and the unification of England and Scotland through the marriage of Mary Queen of Scots and the young Prince Edward. It is doubted by most historians that Henry VIII, even if he had lived, would have been successful, because the cost of the war had already crippled the country's finances. Somerset was faced with the problems of establishing a regency government for the young Edward VI, pacifying the religious factions and finding additional money to continue the war. After the fall of Somerset in 1550, Northumberland, in addition to having to restore order after the popular uprisings of 1549, was confronted with the same difficulties. Furthermore, the situation had deteriorated to such an extent that he had little choice but to make peace with France and Scotland, and adopt a policy of weak neutrality. After 1553, Mary's devotion to the Catholic and Habsburg cause is seen as making it almost inevitable that English foreign policy would be dictated by her forceful husband, Philip II of Spain.

*Even without these internal difficulties, few historians consider that England could have played anything more than a minor role in mid-sixteenth-century western European diplomacy. As a small off-shore island, England had neither the resources nor the manpower to compete with great continental powers such as France, Spain, or the Holy Roman Empire. Paradoxically, it is this very situation that is seen as averting the real threat of foreign invasion. The Habsburg rulers of the Empire and Spain and the Valois kings of France were so well matched in their struggle for power that neither of them could afford to launch an invasion of England. At the same time, the Scots were not strong enough to pose a serious threat, and the French could not risk diverting enough troops to do more than help the Scots prevent an English conquest. Thus, any uneasy balance of power maintained the status quo.

*In many respects the mid-sixteenth century is considered to mark a watershed, or turning-point, in western European diplomacy. The abdication of Charles V in 1555 brought about the break-up of the Empire, which was divided between Charles' son Philip and his brother Ferdinand. To the east of the Rhine, the new emperor, Ferdinand, was preoccupied with the religious quarrel among the German princes and the advance of the Ottoman Turks along the river Danube. In the west, Philip II of Spain was to become increasingly concerned about stamping out heresy in his territories, and checking the growth of Ottoman seapower in the Mediterranean. In the 1560s France was to be plunged into religious civil war. The struggle between the forces of the Reformation and the Counter Reformation would soon overshadow the dynastic wars of the first half of the century. In economic terms the centre of power was moving away from the Mediterranean towards the Atlantic and north western Europe. The loss of Calais in 1558 can be seen to have effectively ended English hopes of regaining her continental empire. After 1558 English foreign policy began to turn away from continental Europe towards the Atlantic and the colonial empires. A new policy was developing, for which control of the sea was of paramount importance. However, in 1547 England was still engaged in a bitter struggle with her neighbours, Scotland and France.

2 Henry VIII's Diplomatic Legacy

England's foreign policy in the mid-sixteenth century, and certainly during the reign of Edward VI, was largely influenced by Henry VIII's diplomacy. Until recently many historians considered that Henry VIII had adopted the principle of holding the balance of power in western Europe. It was thought that in order to achieve this he allied with the weaker nations against the stronger to prevent any one country from becoming too powerful. Modern historians are sceptical about this theory. It is now believed that Henry allied with whichever side was most likely to win – and so help his dynastic ambitions. Henry's foreign policy seems to have been based on three main objectives: to regain the throne of France and outshine his great rival Francis I; to protect English cloth exports to the Netherlands by remaining on good terms with the Holy Roman Empire; and to gain greater control over Scotland, possibly by uniting the two countries. Until the 1530s, when the English Reformation had soured relations with the Catholic Empire, the most useful ally in attempting to achieve these aims had been the Emperor Charles V.

*By 1542, mutual fears over France had restored good relations between England and the Empire. In particular, Henry VIII had seen the Franco-Scottish alliance, created by the marriage of James V and Mary of Guise in 1538, as a major threat to English security. Moreover, he appears to have been becoming increasingly concerned over the succession. Historians are divided about Henry's intentions at this

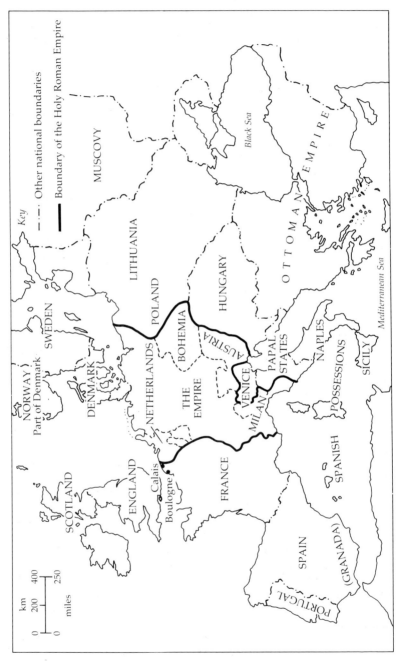

Europe c.1550

stage. It is felt by some that his main aim was to unite Britain by the conquest of Scotland. Others think that he was more concerned with his earlier ambition of claiming the French throne, or, at least, reconquering some of the former English territories on the continent. In 1542 an alliance was agreed by which there was to be a joint Anglo-Imperial invasion of France. This alarmed the Scots, who began to launch raids across the border into England. Henry sent a strong army under the Duke of Norfolk into Scotland, and the Scots were decisively defeated at the Battle of Solway Moss in November 1542. This Scottish reverse was followed by the death of James V in December. Mary of Guise was left as regent for the infant Mary Queen of Scots, and was forced to make peace by the Treaty of Greenwich in 1543, under which the Scots had to agree to a marriage engagement between Mary and Henry's son Edward.

Mary of Guise and the Catholic party in Scotland soon repudiated the marriage agreement. In 1544 and 1545 Henry sent Edward Seymour (later to become the Duke of Somerset) to ravage the Scottish Lowlands. This 'rough wooing' did little to encourage the Scots to support the marriage proposals. At the same time an English army had landed in France to support an invasion by Charles V. This meant that England had to fight a war on two fronts. Consequently, Seymour was given too few troops to do anything effective in Scotland, while the English army in France was too small to do more than capture the port of Boulogne. Even so the cost of the war was enormous, and by 1546 over two million pounds, mainly raised by the sale of monastic lands, had been spent. Charles V withdrew from the war and Henry VIII, plagued by ill health and worried about the cost of the war, was left to make peace with France. It was agreed, under the terms of the Treaty of Campe (sometimes known as the Treaty of Ardres) in June 1546, that England should hold Boulogne for eight years.

*When Henry VIII died in 1547 he left behind him a very uncertain diplomatic situation. The uneasy peace with France and Scotland was further undermined by the renewal of the Franco-Scottish alliance, which left England exposed to the danger of invasion from both north and south. England was in a precarious position, especially as the succession of the young Edward VI, a minor, could be exploited by the two main continental powers to strengthen their own positions in their dynastic wars. Furthermore, the Catholic nations were watching with interest to see if the religious compromise in England would survive the death of Henry VIII. Lord Paget, England's ablest diplomat, summed up the whole position very clearly for the new Regency Council. He thought that England was not strong enough to defend Calais and Boulogne against the French. On the other hand Charles V was a threat because of his support for the Catholic religion. However, he felt that it was too dangerous for England to risk assisting the Lutheran princes in Germany. Consequently he recommended that the alliance with Charles

V should be maintained, and that all efforts should be made to promote hostility between France and the Holy Roman Empire.

3   Edward VI and Somerset 1547–9

Foreign policy during the first part of Edward VI's reign was strongly influenced by the situation left by Henry VIII. The young King's minority created fears over national security and the succession. There were major concerns over the possibility of renewed French intervention in Scotland and the end of the fragile peace. Affairs in Scotland were of paramount importance because of Henry VIII's desire to see his son Edward married to the infant Mary Queen of Scots. Under the terms of his Will (see page 22) Henry had set aside the Scottish claim to the English throne. This might be seen as a way of encouraging the Scots to accept the proposed marriage between Edward and Mary. On the other hand, Mary Queen of Scots, as a legitimate claimant to the throne, could be used by either the French or the Habsburgs as a means of gaining control of England in the cause of the Catholic faith.

* Somerset decided to try to isolate the Scots by negotiating with France for a defensive alliance. However, the death of Francis I and the

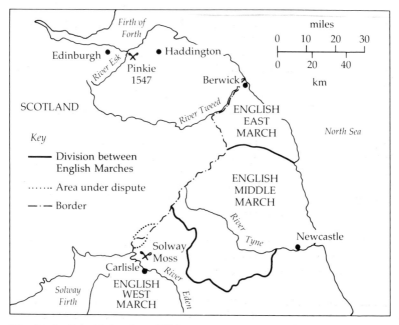

The Anglo-Scottish border c.1550

accession of the more aggressive Henry II ended any hopes of a compromise with the French. Somerset strengthened the defences at Calais, Boulogne and Newhaven, and the fleet was sent to patrol the English Channel. Henry II renewed the Franco-Scottish alliance, and in June 1547 sent a fleet of galleys with 4,000 troops to Scotland. Somerset was left with no alternative but to intervene directly in Scottish affairs on the pretext of arranging the marriage between Edward and Mary agreed in 1543. In September 1547 a joint land and naval invasion of Scotland was launched. Somerset and Dudley led an army to Berwick. They invaded Scotland with 16,000 infantry and 4,000 mercenary cavalry, well supplied with cannon. They were supported at sea by a fleet of 30 warships and 50 supply ships under Lord Clinton. In the west Lord Wharton raided in Scotland from Carlisle with 2,000 troops supported by 500 cavalry. The Scots under Lord Arran raised a militia army of 20,000 troops, but it was poorly equipped with cannon and had only 1,500 light cavalry. The main English army occupied Preston Pans and advanced towards Edinburgh to confront the Scots, who held a strong defensive position on the River Esk. On 10 September the Scots crossed the river to attack the English. At the battle of Pinkie they were cut to pieces by the English cannon and cavalry. After this victory Somerset was able to occupy all the main border strongholds. This gave England control of the border, but the success was not as decisive as it appeared because the English army was not strong enough to occupy the rest of Scotland. In any case, Somerset was anxious about domestic affairs in England, and left Scotland with his main army on 18 September.

* Defeat united the quarrelsome Scottish nobles, and they supported Mary of Guise and her councillors in their opposition to England. While Somerset was in London, the Scottish Council met at Stirling and decided to ask the French for more help. It was suggested that, in return for French military aid, Mary Queen of Scots should marry Henry II's eldest son Francis. Meanwhile England continued to negotiate with France. However, it soon became obvious that war would break out and that France was going to intervene in Scotland. English and French privateers attacked shipping in the English Channel and the North Sea, and the French began to build up their forces around Boulogne. In January 1548 Somerset issued an appeal to the Scots proposing a union between the two countries:

1 Who hath read the histories of time past doth mark and note the great battles fought betwict England and Scotland, the incursions, raids and spoils which hath been done on both parties . . . and shall perceive . . . that of all nations in the world that nation
5 only beside England speaketh the same language, and as you and we be annexed and joined in one island, so no people so like in manner, form, language, and all conditions as we are; shall not he

think it a thing very unmeet, unnatural, and unchristian that
there should be between us so mortal war, who in respect of all
10 other nations be, and should be, like us two bretheren of one
island of Great Britain?
... We offer equality and amity, we overcome in war and offer
peace, we win [strong]holds and offer no conquest, we get in your
land and offer England. What can be more offered and more
15 proffered than the intercourse of merchandise, intercourse of
marriages, the abolishing of all such our laws as prohibiteth the
same or might be impediment to the mutual amity . . . We intend
not to disinherit your Queen but to make her heirs inheritors also
to England. What greater honour can you seek unto your Queen
20 than the marriage offered? What more meet marriage than this
with the King's Highness of England?

For religious and political reasons the Scots preferred the French
option. In June a French fleet landed an army of 10,000 troops in
Scotland, and by August Mary Queen of Scots had been taken to
France to be educated. Henry II proclaimed that France and Scotland
were one country.
    * Meanwhile Somerset remained in London preoccupied with domes-
tic issues. Although Carlisle, Berwick and Haddington Castle, the main
English base north of the border (see the map on page 52), were
strengthened, Somerset seemed unwilling to take any decisive action.
Lord Wharton, the Warden of the West March at Carlisle, and Lord
Grey, Warden of the East March at Berwick, continued to hold the
border with an army of 10,000 troops. However, without instructions
from London, neither of them were prepared to take any initiatives.
This encouraged the French troops in Scotland, reinforced with 8,000
Scots, to besiege Haddington, which had a garrison of 5,000 men. This
placed Somerset in a dilemma. He was unwilling to leave London, and
was worried by the French build-up of forces around Boulogne.
Finally, judging correctly that Henry II would not attack Boulogne for
fear of drawing Charles V into the war, he sent the Earl of Shrewsbury
north with 12,000 infantry and 1,800 cavalry to relieve Haddington.
Shrewsbury succeeded in forcing the besiegers to retreat, but Somerset
soon ordered him to withdraw because of the high cost of maintaining
his army. The siege was resumed, but after unsuccessfully assaulting
the castle in October, the French began to tire of the expense of the
war. In any case the Scottish nobles had begun to resent the French
presence in Scotland, and Franco-Scottish relations deteriorated.
    In January 1549 Somerset decided that Lord Wharton and Lord
Grey were failing to take advantage of this situation. They were
replaced by Lord Dacre and the Earl of Rutland, while the Earl of
Shrewsbury was made Lord President of the Council in the North.
However, before these changes had had time to take effect, affairs in

the north were overshadowed by the peasant uprisings in England. Here again Somerset showed indecision. He was unwilling to withdraw troops from the border garrisons, and this delay allowed the situation in England to get out of control. Finally in August he was forced to withdraw troops from the north, and to recall the fleet to guard the English Channel against possible French attack. This caused the English to abandon Haddington and the other strongholds north of the border. Fortunately for England the French had already decided that the war in Scotland was too costly, and had redeployed their forces on the siege of Boulogne. Without support the Scots were too weak to launch any major attack on the north of England.

*Opinion among historians in their judgement of Somerset as a diplomat and a military commander is divided. It is widely agreed that although he was a good field general, as a Commander-in-Chief he was indecisive and afraid to delegate authority. He is seen as having failed to take advantage of his victory at the Battle of Pinkie, and showed little initiative in pressing home his dominant position along the border. Equally, it is agreed that it was Somerset's military indecision and his unwillingness to redeploy his troops in 1549 that allowed the popular uprisings to get out of hand; not, as it was once maintained, his humanitarian love of the common people. However, some historians consider that Somerset was not altogether to blame for the failure of his foreign policy. It is suggested that he had inherited an almost impossible diplomatic and military position in 1547. He was bound by Henry VIII's Will to arrange a marriage between Edward VI and Mary Queen of Scots in order to safeguard the English succession. In view of the hostility created by Henry VIII's earlier campaigns against the Scots, it is considered to be inevitable that Somerset would have been forced into war with Scotland to achieve this objective. It is also suggested that, given the Franco-Scottish alliance, England's weak military position in France, and the chronic shortage of money, this was a war which could not be won.

4 Edward VI and Northumberland 1550–3

Whatever view is taken of Somerset, it is true that by the autumn of 1549 foreign and domestic affairs had reached a crisis point. The increasing Protestantism of the Church of England had alienated Charles V, and had left England in a very exposed position without a powerful continental ally. Attempts to enforce the agreed marriage between Mary Queen of Scots and Edward VI had not only failed, but had pushed Scotland into a marriage alliance with France. England was committed to a ruinously expensive war on two fronts, the cost of which was adding to the already serious problems at home. Henry II was not slow to take advantage of Somerset's difficulties. He declared war in August and took personal command of the siege of Boulogne. Somerset's failure to deal with all these problems led to his fall, and gave John Dudley the opportunity to seize power.

*During the winter of 1549, while Dudley was engaged in the political struggle to gain control of the Privy Council, the French built up their forces around Boulogne. They were able to break English lines of communication between Boulogne and Calais, which threatened to isolate the garrison of Boulogne under the command of Lord Huntingdon. However, an English fleet decisively defeated a strong force of French galleys in a battle off the Channel Islands. This gave England control of the Channel, and meant that Boulogne could be supplied by sea. Nevertheless, as England was bankrupt, Dudley was unable to raise an army to lift the siege. Attempts to persuade Charles V to extend the treaty protecting Calais to Boulogne failed. Even so, Henry II was afraid that Charles V would intervene to help England. Dudley was keen to end the war so that he could consolidate his own position. In January 1550 a delegation led by Lord Russell was sent to France to negotiate peace. They proposed that in return for ceding Boulogne the French should pay a full ransom, and re-open negotiations about a marriage between Mary Queen of Scots and Edward VI. Henry II took full advantage of England's weak position and refused to make any concessions. Finally, Dudley, strongly supported by Paget, persuaded the Privy Council that they had no alternative but to accept the French terms. The Treaty of Boulogne was signed on 28 March 1550. Under the terms of the Treaty the English had to withdraw from Boulogne in return for a ransom of 400,000 crowns. At the same time they had to remove their remaining garrisons from Scotland, and agree not to renew the war unless provoked by the Scots. Finally, there was to be a perpetual defensive alliance between England and France. Boulogne was handed over to the French on 25 April, and the English garrison was sent to reinforce Calais.

*Although the Treaty of Boulogne removed the danger of French invasion and ended the crippling expense of the war, the potential crisis still remained. The humiliating peace and alliance with a traditional enemy was seen as a national disgrace, and added to Dudley's unpopularity. In spite of this, Dudley negotiated with the French for a marriage between Edward VI and Henry II's daughter Elizabeth. It was agreed that Elizabeth would come to England when she was twelve years of age, and would have a dowry of 200,000 crowns. The alliance was ratified in December 1550, in return for English neutrality in continental wars. England's international position was still very weak, and was made worse because lack of money forced Dudley to run down both the army and the navy. The Habsburgs remained hostile, particularly as the Church of England was beginning to swing towards more extreme Calvinist doctrines (see Chapter 4). In many respects England had returned to the position of weakness and isolation which had resulted from the failure of Henry VIII's foreign policy in 1528.

Certainly the Treaty of Boulogne marked the end of the phase of policy initiated by Henry VIII, during which the reconquest of French territories was a major goal.
*England's relations with the Holy Roman Empire deteriorated steadily. Apart from disliking the Anglo-French alliance, Charles V was particularly annoyed by the attempts of the English reformers to force Princess Mary to abandon her Catholic faith. A consequence of this cooling of relations was a breakdown in commercial contacts with the Netherlands, which had been protected by the *Intercursus Magnus* since 1496. In April 1550 Charles issued an edict allowing the Catholic Inquisition to arrest any heretics in the Netherlands. This outraged many English merchants. Although the edict was modified to exclude foreigners, it helped to bring about the collapse of the Antwerp cloth market, as many Flemish clothworkers fled to England to avoid persecution. The situation was further complicated by disputes over piracy in the English Channel. It was not until December 1550 that Charles made any attempt to restore good trading relations, and then only from fear that England would be driven into a closer alliance with France.

*Anglo-Scottish relationships were in an equally poor state. When Dudley withdrew the remaining English garrisons from Scotland he left the French in total control. However, the Scottish nobles and the Protestant Lowlanders were becoming increasingly hostile towards the French, fearing that Scotland would become a mere province of France. The fall of Somerset had left a confused situation on the English side of the border. Lord Dacre held Carlisle and the Earl of Rutland at Berwick had no clear policy to follow. In 1550 Dudley decided to take personal control of affairs along the border by making himself General Warden of the North, with Lord Wharton as his deputy. To end the constant minor disputes which threatened the uneasy peace, Sir Robert Bowen was ordered to survey the border. He reported that an area fifteen miles by four miles was under dispute. After strengthening Berwick and Carlisle, Dudley returned to London, leaving Lord Dacre to negotiate a settlement of the line of the border with the Scottish wardens. Progress was very slow, and it was not until a French fleet landed supplies and troops in Scotland in February 1551 that negotiations began in earnest. Finally, in March 1552, it was agreed that the border was to be restored to the line held before Henry VIII's Scottish campaigns.

*During 1551 Dudley maintained his policy of neutrality towards the continental powers. Charles V continued to disapprove of the increasing Protestantism of the Church of England, and considered that English foreign policy was unpredictable. It was not until March 1552, when war broke out again between Charles V and Henry II, that Anglo-Imperial relations began to improve. Dudley resisted French pressure to join in the war against the Holy Roman Empire, and

Charles V was more conciliatory over English trade with the Netherlands. Finally, by June 1552, good diplomatic relations were restored between the two countries. Then, when the French invaded Lorraine and the Netherlands, Charles V reminded England that she was bound under treaty obligations to assist the Empire if the Netherlands were attacked. The garrison at Calais was reinforced, but England still took no active part in the war. Even so, England's relations with France deteriorated. The second half of the ransom for Boulogne remained unpaid and French privateers had begun to attack English shipping. Although England was in no position to take any military action, the French feared an Anglo-Imperial alliance and were careful to avoid open confrontation. In January, Dudley, now Duke of Northumberland, proposed to act as mediator between France and the Empire. This action was prompted by fears over Edward VI's declining health and the illness of Charles V. The French were not interested in making peace, and in June 1553 the negotiations collapsed.

*The decline of the Antwerp cloth market and the breakdown in commercial relations with the Empire prompted English merchants to urge the government to find new markets. In 1547 the Italian explorer, Sebastion Cabot, had been given a pension of £100 a year to live in England and help to discover new lands. In 1551 William Hawkins opened up trade in cloth, timber, saltpetre, iron and sugar along the Barbary coast. By 1553 English ships were trading as far as the Gold Coast in West Africa. English merchants were eager to break into the trade with the Far East; their ships and their navigation, however, were too poor to attempt the sea routes around the Cape of Good Hope. In any case, until after 1558, successive English governments did not encourage Atlantic exploration for fear of offending Spain and endangering the Anglo-Habsburg alliance. To overcome these difficulties the cartographer and geographer, John Dee, proposed finding a north-east passage to the East. In 1552 a joint-stock company was established with Sebastion Cabot as its governor, to which city merchants and members of the Privy Council each contributed £25. In May 1553 Sir Hugh Willoughby was put in command of three ships, and given sailing orders drawn up by Sebastion Cabot. The Privy Council gave Willoughby letters of introduction to the ruler of China. Willoughby and two of the ships were lost in Lapland in 1554. His second-in-command, Richard Chancellor, succeeded in reaching the port of Archangel in the White Sea and established diplomatic links with Ivan IV, the Tsar of Muscovy. In 1555 the Muscovy Company was founded to establish trade between the two countries (see page 137). This early English exploration, and improvements to the dockyards and the navy begun in 1555, were to come to fruition later during the reign of Elizabeth I.

*At the time these events were overshadowed by the death of Edward VI in 1553, and the ensuing constitutional crisis. Obviously the question of the succession in England was of great interest to both Charles V and Henry II. The accession of the Catholic Mary Tudor, with her strong attachment to the Habsburgs, would probably bring England into the war on the imperial side. Charles V was strongly in favour of this solution, which would enhance his war effort and restore Catholicism in England. From the French point of view this would have been a far from ideal situation. Consequently they favoured a succession that would leave Northumberland in power, and possibly produce a situation where they could intervene in favour of the claims of Mary Queen of Scots. Although the imperial diplomats were convinced that Mary Tudor's claim to the throne would be ignored, Northumberland's plans to replace her with Lady Jane Grey failed because of lack of support among the English aristocracy and gentry (see page 37).

*Historians have revised their opinion of Northumberland as a diplomat. In the past he has been seen in the same light as by his contemporaries; as a man who betrayed the national honour by giving Boulogne back to France and then adopting a policy of cowardly appeasement. Recently historians have begun to see him not only as a good soldier, but also as a quite capable diplomat. They consider that, faced as he was by an impossible military situation and a bankrupt Exchequer, he was taking the only sensible course by making peace. With Mary Queen of Scots safely in France, it is felt that there would have been little point in prolonging hostilities with Scotland. Furthermore, Northumberland is seen as taking decisive action by assuming personal control as Lord Warden to investigate the petty disputes along the Scottish border. He is also seen to have possessed the ability to delegate authority, by leaving Lord Dacre, with his wide experience of northern affairs, to reach a final settlement. It is suggested that the ceding of Boulogne was equally pragmatic. Historians now consider that, even with the support of the Habsburgs, England would not have been able to hold Boulogne – a town which, apart from being a symbol of national prestige, was of no real value to the country.

5 Mary Tudor 1553–8

As expected, Mary's successful bid for the throne once again placed England securely in alliance with the Holy Roman Empire. Her proposed marriage with Philip of Spain, Charles V's eldest son, meant that England would be firmly allied with the most powerful country in western Europe. Moreover, as the Netherlands were to form part of Philip's inheritance, England's main commercial outlet would be secure. However, in spite of these apparent advantages, many Englishmen feared that the alliance would lead to war with France. There were similar fears in France, and the French ambassador, Noailles, worked hard to promote opposition to the marriage. He was certainly involved in the conspiracy to marry Courtenay to Princess Elizabeth and place them both on the throne (see page 41). That the government was well aware of these problems and their implications is clear from a report in November 1553 to Charles V from Simon Renard about a conversation between Mary, Lord Paget and Renard concerning the English succession.

1 The rival claimants would be the Queen of Scotland, the affianced bride of the Dauphin, who had a real right by descent; the Lady Frances, wife of the Duke of Suffolk, who would also have a claim if the Queen of Scotland were excluded as having been born
5 abroad, as being a Scotswoman and married to the Dauphin of France; and my Lady Elizabeth, who claimed the crown because of the disposition of the late King Henry, authorised by an act of Parliament that had never been repealed ... As for the Lady Elizabeth, the Queen would scruple to allow her to succeed
10 because of her heretical opinions, illegitimacy, and characteristics in which she resembled her mother; and as her mother had caused great trouble in the kingdom, the Queen feared that Elizabeth might do the same, and particularly that she would imitate her mother in being a French partisan ... But [if Mary died childless]
15 it seemed to him [Paget] that, as Parliament had accepted the Lady Elizabeth as proper to succeed, it would be difficult to deprive her of the right she claimed without causing trouble.

The failure of the plot, and the defeat of Wyatt in Kent, ended French hopes of preventing the Anglo-Spanish alliance. Although the marriage agreement appeared to safeguard England against being involved in Philip's wars, there was a clause which stipulated that Philip should aid Mary in governing her kingdom. This provided a loophole which Philip could use to draw England into the continental conflict.

By July 1555 it had become apparent that Mary was not going to bear any children and that her health was deteriorating, so ending Philip II's hopes of an heir to rule in England. In October, still plagued by ill-health, Charles V abdicated his titles and went into retirement at the age of 55. His brother Ferdinand succeeded to his German lands, while Philip became King of Spain and ruler of the Netherlands, Naples, Sicily, Milan and the New World. Philip left England to assume his new responsibilities. However, Stephen Gardiner, the most trusted of Mary's English councillors, died in November 1555, and she was anxious for Philip to return to England to advise her. He paid little attention to her pleas until March 1556, when the war with France broke out again. Philip came to England to enlist support, but the Privy Council was totally opposed to any involvement in the war. England was still in a weak military position in spite of reforms to the army and navy (see page 44). Then, however, fresh French plots against Mary came to light, and the Privy Council reluctantly declared war on France. In July 1556 the Earl of Pembroke was sent to France with an army of 7,000 men. There they joined the army commanded by Philibert, Duke of Savoy, who won a decisive victory over the French at St Quentin in 1557. At the same time the English fleet attacked the French coast. These combined operations forced the Duke of Guise, commanding the main French army, to return to France from Italy. In retaliation for the English intervention he launched an attack on Calais. Unfortunately the government had already been forced to borrow heavily to equip the army and navy sent to the continent, and were unable to afford to send reinforcements to Calais. The defences of Calais had been neglected, and Lord Wentworth, the commander, was unable to make any real resistance. Calais fell on 13 January 1558, and the French soon occupied the remainder of the English strongholds around the port.

In response to this humiliating defeat the government raised an army of 7,000 troops, supported by a fleet of 140 ships, to invade France. The intention was not to recapture Calais, but to attack Brest. Finding Brest too heavily defended the English force captured the smaller port of Le Conquet. Meanwhile Henry II and Philip II were camped near Amiens with armies of 45,000 men. Instead of the expected decisive battle, the two monarchs decided to negotiate. At first Philip demanded the return of Calais to England as part of the settlement. Then Mary died in November 1558, and Philip abandoned his former ally. Under the terms of the Peace of Cateau-Cambresis in April 1559 France and Spain signed a lasting peace treaty. Philip married Henry II's daughter Elizabeth, and the French guaranteed not to intervene in Philip's Italian territories. France retained Calais, the last English possession on the continent.

Although historians no longer agree with the opinion of Mary's contemporaries that the loss of Calais was a national disaster, they continue to condemn her conduct of foreign affairs. It is still considered that Mary's stubbornness, and her almost total reliance on her Spanish advisers, made England's military débâcle between 1557 and 1558 almost inevitable. There is some sympathy for Mary over the way in which Philip II blatantly used England for his own ends, but it is felt that she was too infatuated with Philip and the Habsburgs to take reasonable precautions to protect English interests. It is thought that in 1553 the Habsburgs had serious intentions of turning England into a permanent base, to complete the 'Habsburg ring' encircling France. Philip's unpopularity in England, and the realisation in 1555 that Mary was incapable of producing an heir, is seen as the reason for abandoning this strategy. This, it is thought, is what convinced Philip in 1556 to use English troops for short-term military gains, and for his desertion of his ally after the death of Mary in 1558.

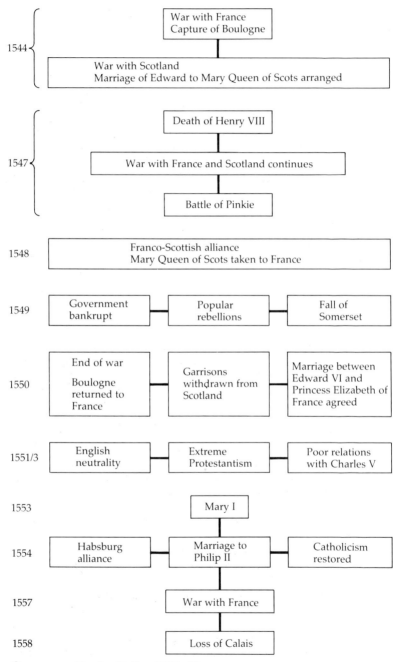

Summary – Foreign Policy 1547–58

Making notes on 'Foreign Policy 1547–58'

This chapter is designed to explore the extent to which English foreign policy was strongly influenced by religion and worries over the succession. English foreign policy between 1547 and 1558 was to a large extent the result of Henry VIII's diplomacy, especially with regard to Scotland, and the long-term struggle between France and the Holy Roman Empire. The new issues of religious differences and the growing conflict between Catholics and Protestants in western Europe were coming to the forefront. You need to decide how important these various issues were in shaping English foreign policy, and how successful the political leaders were in maintaining England's diplomatic position. The following headings, sub-headings and questions should help you:

1.   Introduction.
1.1.   Why were Somerset and Northumberland faced by an almost impossible diplomatic situation?
1.2.   Why was a pro-Habsburg policy almost inevitable under Mary I?
1.3.   Was the mid-sixteenth century a 'watershed' in western European diplomacy?
2.   Henry VIII's Diplomatic Legacy.
2.1.   What were Henry VIII's main diplomatic objectives?
2.2.   Why and with what success did Henry VIII go to war with France and Scotland in 1542 and 1544?
2.3.   What diplomatic problems did Henry VIII leave his successors?
3.   Edward VI and Somerset 1547–9.
3.1.   Why was Mary Queen of Scots so important to English foreign policy?
3.2.   Why and with what success did Somerset invade Scotland in 1547?
3.3.   Why did the Scots reject the idea of union with England?
3.4.   How successful was Somerset in maintaining control in Scotland, and why was he finally forced to withdraw troops from Scotland and France in 1549?
3.5.   How do historians now assess Somerset as a diplomat and a military commander?
4.   Edward VI and Northumberland 1550–3.
4.1.   Why had foreign affairs reached a crisis point by the autumn of 1549?
4.2.   Why did Northumberland make peace with France in 1550?
4.3.   Why was England's diplomatic position still weak after peace had been made?
4.4.   Why did relations with Charles V deteriorate?
4.5.   How successful was Northumberland in settling affairs in Scotland?

4.6. Why did relations with the Holy Roman Empire improve in 1552–3?

4.7. Why did England become more interested in exploration after 1553?

4.8. What diplomatic changes were created by the death of Edward VI?

4.9. How do historians assess Northumberland as a diplomat?

5. Mary Tudor 1553–8.

5.1. What was the effect of Mary's reign on English foreign policy?

Answering essay questions on 'Foreign Policy 1547–58'

1. 'Explain the changes in England's foreign policy that took place following the accession of Mary I.'
2. 'Assess the degree of success of England's foreign policy between 1547 and 1588.'
3. '"Somerset fell from power largely because he was unsuccessful in foreign policy." Discuss.'

Two of these questions require answers that concentrate on foreign affairs. Which question does not? Which question requires you to distinguish between Somerset's and Northumberland's dealings in foreign affairs?

Both of questions 1 and 2 could be answered using a country by country approach. Which countries would form your paragraph points in each case? In what order would you arrange your paragraphs? Why? It would be sensible to explain your criteria for choosing your paragraph order. Where would you do this? Think of two other approaches to answering question 2 (clues: personalities and degree of success). Make a detailed plan for one of these approaches.

Source-based questions on 'Foreign Policy 1547–58'

1 Relations with Scotland
Read the extract from Somerset's Epistle of Exhortation to the Scots (January 1548), given on pages 53–4. Answer the following questions:
a) What is meant by 'intercourse of merchandise' (line 15)? (1 mark)
b) Explain the significance of the offer of 'intercourse of marriages' (line 15). (3 marks)
c) Explain in detail Somerset's assertion that 'no people [are] so like in

manner, form, language, and all conditions as we are'. (8 marks)

d) What proposal was Somerset making to the Scots? (3 marks)

e) What were the consequences of the Scottish decision not to accept the English proposal? (5 marks)

2 Renard on the English succession, 1553

Read the extract from Renard's report to Charles V, given on page 60, and answer the following questions:

a) What is meant by 'scruple' (line 9)? (1 mark)

b) What three reasons does Renard give as the basis of a possible rejection of the claim of Mary Queen of Scots to the succession? (3 marks)

c) What evidence might Renard have presented to suggest that Paget's prediction was sound? (4 marks)

d) What was Renard's purpose in writing his report? What are the implications of this for its likely accuracy? (6 marks) ·

e) Why was the English succession of interest to Charles V? Support your answer with evidence from outside the extract. (6 marks)

CHAPTER 4

Religious Change 1547–58

1 Introduction

Views among historians about the significance of religion in mid-Tudor England have changed during recent years. It is now felt that there was a much greater degree of religious compromise in England than on the continent, and that as a result religion itself was not a cause of crisis. However, religion is seen as having a considerable influence on the political, social and economic changes which were taking place at the time. Consequently, religion can be seen as contributing directly, or indirectly, to potential crises, such as in the Western Rebellion of 1549, or in the attempt by Northumberland to stop Mary Tudor succeeding to the throne in 1553.

In the past, historians saw the Edwardian Reformation as a period of remarkable toleration during which reformed religion became firmly established in the country. They saw it as being followed by five years of Catholic repression and persecution, which failed to stamp out English Protestantism. Such views are no longer widely held. It is increasingly doubted whether Protestantism had taken much of a hold in England by 1553. At the same time, it is now thought that there was much less animosity between English Catholics and Protestants than was previously believed. It is true that there were extremists on both sides, just as there were individuals prepared to die for their faith. However, the vast majority of people are seen as being very moderate in their outlook, and as being prepared to accept whatever doctrine was held by the ruling regime. It is this that is seen as being the basis for religious compromise in England. The whole of the period between 1547 and 1553 is held to be one of marked toleration. Even the Marian religious repression is regarded as very mild in comparison with the persecution on the continent.

*At the same time religion had become a political issue. There is wide agreement among historians that Henry VIII's motives in breaking away from Rome were much more political than religious. The English Reformation put the Church firmly under the control of the State. It also removed England from the authority of the Pope; a source of outside interference which was highly resented among the English élites. Ecclesiastical wealth replenished the Exchequer, which had been almost bankrupted by Henry VIII's unsuccessful wars of the 1520s. On the surface the Crown was the main beneficiary of the English Reformation. Yet, once religion had come to the forefront of the political arena, it created problems for the monarchy. Religious differences deepened the rift between political factions at Court. Henry VIII had to tread a cautious path between the conservative Catholic and reforming Protestant parties. The care with which he tried, in his Will of 1547, to balance the two religious parties in the Regency Council, shows the importance he gave to religion as an issue in domestic politics.

In 1549 the fall of Somerset led to a renewed power struggle, which ended with the leading conservatives being expelled from the Privy Council. Northumberland's attempt to change the succession in 1553 was prompted not only by personal ambition, but also by the desire to prevent the Catholics regaining power under Mary Tudor. Even so there was still a great deal of toleration. A majority of the ruling élites favoured moderate reform, but Catholic politicians were not excluded from government purely for religious reasons. Stephen Gardiner, the leading Catholic bishop, spent most of Edward VI's reign in prison, but this was largely because he refused to cooperate in any way with the Privy Council. When Mary Tudor came to power in 1553 there was no great purge of Protestant politicians. Indeed, men like Paget were given high office. It is true that Mary did not trust such men, but neither did she have great confidence in her English Catholic councillors. Given that moderates were in a majority, the fact that Mary came to the throne at all is a sign of the toleration in England. She was supported as the legitimate heir in spite of her religion. During her reign most politicians and civil servants were prepared to conform to her religious views. It was not her religion, but the ending of the royal supremacy and her marriage to Philip II of Spain that provoked most opposition.

*Religious differences made politics and diplomacy much more complicated. Religion had become an important diplomatic issue in foreign affairs in western Europe. This meant that English foreign and domestic policy had to avoid antagonising the major continental powers. For this reason the question of the English succession became a matter of international interest. It was partly fear over the succession and the threat of Catholic intervention that prompted Henry VIII to go to war with Scotland and France in 1542 and 1544. He failed to achieve his aim of uniting England and Scotland through the marriage of Prince Edward and Mary Queen of Scots. Somerset tried to force the Scots into agreeing to the marriage by continuing the war. The failure of this plan led to bankruptcy in 1549, and forced Northumberland into making peace and maintaining a policy of weak neutrality. Moreover, the Catholic powers on the continent were able to use Mary Queen of Scots, as a legitimate Catholic claimant to the English throne, as an excuse to intervene in English affairs, particularly under Elizabeth I.

Religion was the cause of other difficulties for English relationships with the continent. England's main ally and trading partner was Charles V. However, Charles was a leading supporter of the Counter Reformation. He was therefore opposed to religious reform in England, fearing that it would lead to a swing towards Protestantism. Consequently, the English Reformation had brought the country to the brink of war with the Holy Roman Empire. Somerset is seen by many historians as being careful to introduce only moderate religious reforms in order to avoid offending Charles V. When Northumberland began to allow the Church of England to become more Calvinist, Charles withdrew his support, so leaving the country in a very weak military and diplomatic position with no major continental ally. During the reign of Mary I England was drawn into a Catholic, Habsburg alliance, which eventually led to war with France and the loss of Calais. However, this must be seen more as a dynastic alliance, with religion playing a secondary role.

2 The Henrician Church in 1547

In order to see the significance of the religious changes which took place between 1547 and 1558 it is necessary to understand the doctrinal position in the Church of England at the death of Henry VIII. From the time that Henry had made himself Head of the English Church in 1534 he was under pressure to formulate an acceptable doctrine. The reform party led by Cranmer had advocated the introduction of moderate Lutheran ideas. On the other hand, the pro-Catholic, conservative faction led by Gardiner had favoured a policy of minimum change to the basic Catholic doctrines. During the period from 1534 to 1546 royal favour swung between the two groups. The first major statement of doctrine, the Act of the Ten Articles, had come in 1536. This Act was passed when the reformers were in the ascendancy, and had introduced more Lutheran doctrines into the Church of England. Three years later the conservatives had regained royal favour, and the Act of the Six Articles had been passed to remove many of the Lutheran beliefs. Such shifts of policy had meant that by 1547 the doctrines of the Church of England were a compromise, and contained many inconsistencies which were unacceptable to reformers and conservatives alike.

*When Henry VIII died the main articles of faith in the Church of England were in line with traditional Catholic orthodoxy. The Eucharist was clearly defined in the Catholic form of transubstantiation – the sacramental bread and wine being transformed at consecration into the body and blood of Christ. The Lutheran form of consubstantiation – the belief that the sacramental bread and wine remained unchanged at communion, but that there was a real presence of Christ in the heart of a true believer – was no longer accepted in the Church of England. Only the clergy were permitted to take communion in both the bread and the wine, while the laity were again restricted to taking only the sacramental bread. The Catholic rites of confirmation, marriage, holy orders and extreme unction had been re-introduced, alongside the previously recognised sacraments of the Eucharist, penance and baptism. The laity were still required to make regular confession of sins to a priest, and to seek absolution and penance. English clergy were no longer allowed to marry, and those who had married before 1540 had had to send away their wives and families, or lose their livings. Although there was no specific statement on the existence of Purgatory, the need for the laity to do 'good works' for their salvation had been reinstated. The singing of masses for the souls of the dead was held to be 'agreeable also to God's Law'. It was for this reason that the chantries, where a priest sang masses for the souls of the founder and his family, were not closed down at the same time as the monasteries. Paintings and statues of the saints were still allowed in the churches, although the laity were instructed not actually to worship them. Many of the processions and rituals of the Catholic Church were still practised, because it was maintained that they created a good religious frame of mind among the congregations.

　* Although the Church of England remained fundamentally Catholic in doctrine, it had adopted a number of Protestant practices by 1547. Services were still conducted in Latin, but Cranmer's English Litany had been authorised in 1545. Greater importance was attached to the sermon, and the Lord's Prayer, the Creed and the Ten Commandments had to be taught in English by parents to their children and servants. Similarly the Great Bible of 1539 was the authorised English translation which replaced the Latin Vulgate Bible. Moreover, the élite laity were allowed to read the Great Bible in their own homes, unlike on the continent where only the Catholic clergy were allowed to read and interpret the Bible. The practice of the Church of England with regard to some Catholic doctrines was ambiguous. Saints could be 'reverenced for their excellent virtue' and could be offered prayers, but the laity were forbidden to make pilgrimages to the shrines of saints or to offer them gifts, because it was maintained that grace, salvation and remission of sins came only from God. At the same time the number of Holy Days – days on which, like Sundays, the laity were expected to attend church and not to work – had been reduced to 25. Finally, in sharp contrast to Catholic countries, there had been no monasteries in England since 1539, when even the larger monasteries had been closed by royal order, and their possessions confiscated to the Crown.

Attempts between 1534 and 1546 to establish a uniform set of articles of faith for the Church of England had only succeeded in producing a patchwork of doctrines that often conflicted. Until 1547 this ramshackle structure was held together by the Henrician treason and heresy laws. Anyone breaking, or even questioning, the statutes and proclamations defining the doctrines of the Church of England was liable to confiscation of property, fines, imprisonment, or execution. Similarly the censorship laws prevented the printing, publishing, or importation of books and pamphlets expressing views contrary to the doctrines of the Church of England.

3 The Edwardian Church 1547–9

The accession of Edward VI, who had been educated as a Protestant, roused the hopes of English reformers that there would be a swing towards more Lutheran, and possibly Calvinist, doctrines. Somerset's appointment as Lord Protector in 1547 brought the reform party firmly into power, and effectively ended Henry VIII's policy of religious compromise. Somerset was a moderate Protestant, but although he was devout, he had no real interest in theology. He was religiously tolerant, and favoured a cautious approach towards reform. Although he is reputed to have had Calvinistic leanings, and, certainly, exchanged letters with John Calvin, there is little evidence of such influences when he was in power. The reformers were in the majority in the Privy Council. However, among the bishops, nine led by Cranmer and Ridley supported reform, while ten led by Gardiner and Edmund Bonner, Bishop of London, opposed change. The remaining eight bishops were undecided on doctrinal issues. But all the bishops fully supported the royal supremacy, and the separation from Rome. With such an even balance of opinion among the bishops the Privy Council moved very cautiously on matters of religious reform.

* The attitude towards reform outside the immediate government circle is difficult to assess. A majority of the élites seems to have been in favour (or at least, not opposed) to some measure of religious reform. In general, however, the lower clergy appear to have been opposed to religious change. This, it has been suggested, was largely because the English parish clergy were still relatively uneducated, and were anxious to maintain their traditional way of life without any complications. It is maintained that the same was true for the great mass of the population, who were very conservative in their outlook. Moreover, as far as they were concerned both their popular culture, which was based on rituals and festivals associated with the farming year, and their belief in magic and witchcraft, all formed part of the ceremonies of the old Church. Yet there were exceptions. In East Anglia, because of the settlement of large numbers of Protestant refugees from the continent, there was considerable support for religious reform. In London and the larger towns, where clergy were better educated, there were very vocal minorities demanding more rapid, and more radical religious change.

* In these circumstances the Privy Council decided to review the state of the Church of England, and to introduce some moderate Protestant reforms. Such a policy was opposed by the conservatives, prompted by Gardiner, who maintained that under the terms of Henry VIII's Will, no religious changes could be made until Edward VI came of age at 18. In spite of Gardiner's vigorous opposition, royal commissioners were sent to visit all the bishoprics. They were instructed to compile a report by the autumn of 1547 on the state of the clergy and the doctrines and practices to be found in every diocese. At the same time, to help the spread of Protestant ideas, every parish was ordered to obtain a copy of Cranmer's *Book of Homilies*, and *Paraphrases* by Erasmus. In July an injunction was issued to the bishops ordering them to instruct their clergy to conduct services in English, and to preach a sermon every Sunday. Furthermore, the bishops were to create libraries of Protestant literature and provide an English Bible for each parish, and to encourage the laity to read these books. Finally the bishops were told to remove all superstitious statues and images from their churches.

These modest moves towards religious reform did not satisfy the more vocal Protestant activists. The amount of anti-Catholic protest was increased by the presence of Protestant exiles who had returned from the continent after the death of Henry VIII. The problem for the Privy Council was that, while it did not wish to introduce reforms too quickly for fear of provoking a Catholic backlash, it was anxious not to prevent religious debate by taking repressive measures. As a result, the Henrician treason, heresy and censorship laws were not enforced and a vigorous debate over religion developed. The more radical reformers launched a strong attack through a pamphlet campaign on both the Catholic Church and the bishops, who were accused of being self-seeking royal servants and not true pastors. Other pamphlets attacked the wealth of the Church, superstitious rituals, and in particular the Eucharist. However, there was no agreement among the protesters about the form of Protestant doctrine that should be adopted. With the government refusing to take any firm lead there was growing frustration, and some of the more radical protesters took matters into their own hands.

In London, East Anglia, Essex and Lincolnshire, where large numbers of Protestant refugees from the continent were settling, riots broke out. These frequently included outbreaks of iconoclasm, in which stained glass windows, statues, and other superstitious images were destroyed. In some cases gold and silver candlesticks and other church plate were seized and sold, with the money being donated to the poor. Such incidents were often provoked by extreme millenarianists, who wished to see a more equal society and a redistribution of wealth to the poor. Although the Privy Council was alarmed by the violence, it refused to take any action against the demonstrators. This inaction enraged the more conservative bishops. Bishop Bonner was particularly vehement in his protests to the government, and was imprisoned for two months.

*When Parliament and Convocation – the assembly of clergy – were summoned in November 1547, the question of religious reform was freely discussed. Both assemblies were in favour of reform, and Convocation agreed to re-introduce clerical marriage, although this was not approved by Parliament and so did not become law. Yet the Privy Council was still reluctant to make any decisive move towards religious reform. The reason for this was that the new regime still felt insecure,

The death-bed of Henry VIII: Edward VI and the Pope c.1548

fearing that any major changes to doctrine might provoke even more unrest, and possibly lead to a fall of the government. The two major pieces of legislation, the Chantries Act and the Treason Act, did little to resolve the doctrinal uncertainties. The Chantries Act, by closing the chantries, merely confirmed legislation already passed in 1545. Although, as in 1545, the main purpose of the Act was to raise money to continue the war with France and Scotland, the reason given was that the chantries were centres of superstition. The Treason Act effectively repealed the Henrician treason, heresy and censorship laws (see page 29). This measure only increased the freedom with which the Protestant activists could discuss and demand radical doctrinal reforms. The immediate result was a renewed spate of pamphlets demanding that the Bible should be recognised as the only true authority for religious belief. At the same time English translations of the writings of Luther and Calvin were being widely circulated.

In January 1548 the Privy Council issued a series of proclamations to try to calm the situation. However, the proclamations indicated no clear policy, and so only added to the confusion. The continued validity of Lent and feastdays was defended. Justices of the Peace and churchwardens were ordered to enforce the existing doctrines of the Church of England, including transubstantiation. On the other hand, instructions were issued to speed up the removal of Catholic images from churches. Such indecision infuriated both reformers and conservatives alike. Finally, in September, the Council forbade all public preaching in the hope of stifling debate.

*When Parliament reassembled in November 1548, Somerset and the Council were in a stronger position after the successful campaign in Scotland (see page 53). For this reason they felt secure enough to take a more positive approach to religious reform. Their objective was to end the uncertainty over religious doctrine. It was hoped that the First Edwardian Act of Uniformity, passed in January 1549, would achieve this:

1 Whereupon his Highness . . . hath appointed the Archbishop of Canterbury and certain of the most learned and discreet bishops, and other learned men of this realm, to consider and ponder the premises [statements]; and thereupon having as well eye or
5 respect to the most sincere and pure Christian religion taught by the Scripture, as to usages in the primitive Church, should draw and make one convenient and meet order, rite and fashion of common and open prayer and administration of the sacraments, to be had and used in his Majesties realm of England and in
10 Wales; to which at this time, by the aid of the Holy Ghost, with one uniform agreement is of them concluded, set forth, and delivered to his Highness, to his great comfort and quietness of mind, in a book entitled, the Book of the Common Prayer and

Administration of the Sacraments, and Other Rites and Cere-
15 monies of the Church, after the use of the Church of England.

The Act officially ordered all the clergy of England and Wales to use
a number of Protestant practices which had been allowed, but not
enforced, during the two previous years. Holy communion (the mass),
matins and evensong were to be conducted in English. The sacraments
were now defined as communion, baptism, confirmation, marriage and
burial. Cranmer adapted the old communion service by adding new
prayers, so that the clergy and the laity could take both the sacramental
bread and the wine. Permission was given once again for the clergy to
marry. Many of the traditional Catholic rituals, which the Protestant
reformers considered to be superstitious, disappeared. The practice of
singing masses for the souls of the dead was no longer approved.
However, there was still no really clear statement on the existence, or
otherwise, of Purgatory. Any form of the worship of saints, although
not banned, was to be discouraged, while the removal of statues,
paintings and other images was encouraged. However, Cranmer's *Book
of Common Prayer* was a mixture of Lutheran and Catholic beliefs. Fast
days were still to be enforced and no change was to be made in the
number of Holy Days. The new communion service followed the order
of the old Latin mass, and the officiating clergy were expected to
continue to wear the traditional robes and vestments. Most important-
ly, no change was made to the doctrine of the Eucharist, which was still
defined in the Catholic terms of transubstantiation. This was a fundamental point that angered many of the more radical reformers, who
continued to urge the government to adopt a more Protestant definition
of the sacrament of communion.

The Privy Council hoped that these cautious measures would satisfy
the majority of moderate reformers, without outraging the Catholic
conservatives. Although any clergy who refused to use the new service
were to be liable to fines and imprisonment, no penalties were to be
imposed on the laity for non-attendance. This can be interpreted as a
hope by the Privy Council that they could coerce the more recalcitrant
minority among the parish clergy, while not antagonising the undecided majority among the laity. The government decided to continue
with its policy of educating the laity in Protestant ideas which it had
introduced in July 1547. Bishops were instructed to carry out visita-
tions to encourage the adoption of the new services, and to test whether
parishioners could recite the Lord's Prayer and the Ten Commandments in English. The effectiveness of either the legislation, or the
education programme, depended on whether the bishops and élites
would enforce them. There was opposition in Cornwall, Devon, Dorset
and Yorkshire. However, most of the country seems to have followed
the lead of the aristocracy and gentry in accepting moderate Protestantism.

*It is difficult to judge to what extent underlying opposition to these changes in religion contributed to the fall of Somerset in 1549. Certainly only the Western Rebellion was directly linked with religion, and even there underlying economic and social discontent played an important part in causing the uprising. To a certain extent the rebels in the west were complaining about enclosures and about the gentry, whom they accused of making use of the Reformation to seize church land for their own enrichment. Such views were held in other areas during the popular uprisings of 1549 (see pages 32 and 111), but only in the West Country was direct opposition to the new Act of Uniformity the central issue.

The popular discontent began in Cornwall in 1547, when the local archdeacon, William Body, who was disliked both for his Protestant views and for his personal greed, began to try to introduce religious reforms. He was mobbed by a hostile crowd at Penryn and fled to London. In April 1548 he returned to Cornwall to supervise the destruction of Catholic images in churches. At Helston Body was set upon, and killed, by a mob led by a local priest. As the troublemakers dispersed quickly the authorities made only a few arrests. But they hanged the ten ringleaders. Then in 1549 the Cornish lower orders, fearing that the Act of Uniformity was going to be imposed on them, rose in rebellion and set up an armed camp at Bodmin. Because of the hostility expressed by the rebels towards landlords, only six of the more Catholic local gentry joined the uprising. However, the West Country élites were very unwilling to take any action against the rebellion on behalf of the government. The main leaders of the rebels were local clergy, and it was they who began to draw up a series of articles listing demands to stop changes in religion. In Devon there was an independent uprising at Sampford Courtenay. By 20 June the Devon and Cornish rebels had joined forces at Crediton, and three days later they set up an armed camp at Clyst St Mary. Local negotiations broke down, and the rebels began to blockade the nearby town of Exeter with an army of 6,000 men. Lord Russell, who had been sent to crush the rebellion, was hampered by a shortage of troops and a lack of local gentry support. As a result it was not until August that the rebels were finally defeated.

* Some of the demands put forward in the final set of articles drawn up by the rebels clearly illustrate their religious conservatism and other grievances felt in the West Country:

1 I. First we will have the general counsel and holy decrees of our
   forefathers observed, kept and performed, and who so ever shall
   speak against them, we hold them as heretics.
   II. Item we will have the Lawes of our Sovereign Lord Kyng
5 Henry the VIII concerning the Six Articles, to be used as they
   were in his time.

III. Item we will have the mass in Latin, as was before, and celebrated by the priest without any man or woman communicating with him.

10 IV. Item we will have the Sacrement hung over the high altar, and there to be worshipped as it used to be, and they whiche will not therto consent, we will have them die like heretics against the holy Catholic faith.

VII. Item we will have holy bread and holy water made every 15 Sunday ... Images to be set up again in every church, and all other ancient olde Ceremonies used as heretofore, by our mother the holy Church.

VIII. Item we will not receive the newe service because it is but lyke a Christmas game ...

20 X. Item we will have the whole Bible and all books of scripture in English to be called in again ...

XIV. Item we will that the halfe parte of the abbey lands and Chantry lands, in every mans possession, howsoever he came by them, be given again to two places, where two of the chief Abbeys 25 used to be in every County ...

The government clearly saw these articles as ultra-conservative demands for a return to Catholicism, and they were vigorously repudiated by Cranmer and the leading theologians among the reformers. It was claimed that the rank and file had been misled by, as Somerset put it, 'seditious priests, to seek restitution of the old bloody laws' for their own purposes. It was the manner in which the articles were phrased, just as much as their content, that offended the government. Unlike the usual wording of petitions to the Crown by rebels, such as the 'We pray your grace' used by Robert Kett in the same year, each of the Western rebels' articles began 'Item we will have'. Such lack of deference and respect, along with denials of the royal supremacy in the articles themselves, was seen as a greater threat to the stability of society and the State than the rebellion itself. Cranmer was particularly enraged by such insubordination, and by the suggestion in article XIII that no gentleman should have more than one servant. It was this that enabled the government to accuse the rebels of being dangerous social anarchists, and so distract attention from their attack on religious change. In any case the government theologians found no difficulty in pouring scorn on the lack of doctrinal knowledge in the articles. Their demands for the return of images and the old ceremonies were dismissed as idolatrous, and the old mass was described as being more like games held during the Christmas season. Even greater scorn was poured on the suggestion in article VIII that they rejected the new services in English because as Cornishmen it was a language that they did not understand. Historians agree that the rebels showed little knowledge of either Protestant or Catholic doctrines, but suggest that such ignorance in the West Country probably reflected similar confusion among the great mass of the population. Whether this is true or not, these demands do show that, in the West Country at least, many of the laity were still strongly attached to the familiar traditions of the old Church.

4 The Edwardian Church 1550-3

When John Dudley, the future Duke of Northumberland, gained power in 1550, religious reform became more radical. It is difficult to decide whether this suggests that the government considered that there was no widespread opposition to religious change, or that they thought that the recent suppression of the popular uprisings was sufficient to prevent any further unrest. Possibly, as is thought by many historians, the changes came about because of political in-fighting in the Privy Council. What is certain is that by 1553 the Church of England had become Protestant.

In view of his reconversion to Catholicism before his execution in 1553, many historians do not think it likely that Dudley was a genuine religious reformer. Other historians feel that his support for such a Protestant enthusiast as John Hooper against Cranmer and Nicholas Ridley, Bishop of London, in the doctrinal dispute during the autumn of 1550 (see page 78) does show that he was interested in religious reform. This is a question which, without fresh evidence, is unlikely to be resolved. Certainly the first moves towards introducing more radical Protestantism seem to have arisen from the political expediencies following Somerset's fall from power. After the arrest of Somerset in October 1549 it appeared that the conservative faction supported by Dudley might seize power. They planned, with the help of Charles V, to make Princess Mary regent for the young Edward VI. However, neither Charles V nor Mary supported the scheme which, in any case, would not have been practical in view of Edward VI's increasing support for Protestantism. Meanwhile, Dudley, having used the conservatives to strengthen his position on the Privy Council, then switched his allegiance to the more radical Protestant reformers. This political struggle with the Privy Council continued when Parliament met in November. Attempts by conservatives to repeal the 1549 Act of Uniformity and strengthen the power of the bishops were defeated. In December Parliament approved measures to speed up the removal of popish images and old service books from the churches, and set up a commission to revise the procedures for the ordination of priests.

By February 1550 Dudley was firmly in control of the Privy Council, and the conservatives were driven out of office (see page 33). To strengthen his position still further and to prevent a possible conservative backlash, Dudley moved against the more conservative of the bishops. Gardiner, the most able of the pro-Catholics, was already imprisoned in the Tower of London. In July he was ordered by the Privy Council to agree to the doctrines of the Church of England. He refused, and was sentenced to stricter terms of confinement. Bishop Bonner of London, already imprisoned by Somerset, was retried and deprived of his diocese. He was replaced by Ridley, then Bishop of Rochester, who was an enthusiastic reformer. During the next year active reformers were appointed as bishops of Rochester, Chichester, Norwich, Exeter and Durham. These changes cleared the way for more sweeping religious reforms. The Catholic laity and clergy, deprived of their main spiritual leaders, offered little opposition, although some pro-Catholic pamphlets were circulated.

*The first move to introduce more radical Protestantism was initiated by Ridley in London, where he ordered all altars to be removed and replaced by communion tables in line with the teachings of the Calvinists and other reformed Churches. In other dioceses the destruction of altars proceeded unevenly, and depended on the attitudes of the local élites and clergy. At the same time the Parliamentary Commission's proposals to change the form of the ordination of priests were introduced, and instructions were issued to enforce the first Act of Uniformity. The new form of ordination, which was basically Lutheran, soon caused controversy. The major change – which empowered priests to administer the sacraments and preach the gospel instead of offering 'sacrifice and [the celebration of] mass both for the living and the dead' – satisfied moderate reformers. It removed the supposedly superstitious references to sacrifice, Purgatory, and prayers for the souls of the dead. However, it did not please some of the more extreme reformers, especially because it made no attempt to remove any of the 16 ceremonial vestments, such as the mitre, cope, tippet, or stole, normally worn by bishops and priests while conducting services. These were regarded as superstitious by many of the reformed Churches, whose clergy wore plain surplices. John Hooper, who had been invited to become Bishop of Gloucester, complained that the form of ordination was still too Catholic and started a fierce dispute with Ridley over the question of vestments. As a result he refused the offered bishopric, and in July he began a campaign of preaching against the new proposals. At first it appeared that Dudley was sympathetic and supported Hooper, but in October he was ordered to stop preaching, and in January 1551 he was imprisoned for failing to comply. Finally he was persuaded to compromise and was made Bishop of Gloucester, where he introduced a vigorous policy of education and reform. But he complained that both laity and clergy were slow to respond.

*During 1551 no new reform measures were introduced, but the way was being prepared for a major overhaul of the Church of England. Cranmer was in the process of revising his *Prayer Book*, to remove the many ambiguities that had caused criticism. Further action was taken against the remaining conservative bishops. Gardiner was finally deprived of the diocese of Winchester in February, and in October reformers were appointed at Worcester and Chichester. These moves ensured that there would be a majority among the bishops to support the programme of religious changes that was being prepared. In October, Dudley, after the re-arrest of Somerset, considered himself in full political control, and confirmed his position by taking the title of Duke of Northumberland.

＊Parliament was assembled in January 1552 and the government embarked upon a comprehensive programme of reform. In order to strengthen the power of the Church of England to enforce doctrinal uniformity, a new Treason Act was passed. This made it an offence to question the royal supremacy, or any of the articles of faith of the English Church. At the same time uncertainties over the number of Holy Days to be recognised was ended by officially limiting them to 25. In March the second Act of Uniformity was passed. Under the new Act it became an offence for both clergy and laity not to attend Church of England services, and offenders were to be fined and imprisoned. Cranmer's new *Book of Common Prayer* became the official basis for the Church of England services, and had to be used by both clergy and laity. The new prayer book was based upon the scriptures, and all traces of Catholicism and the mass had been removed. The Eucharist was clearly defined in terms of consubstantiation (see page 68), although there are some suggestions that Cranmer was moving towards a more Zwinglian, or Calvinistic definition of the Eucharist as commemorative of Christ's sacrifice, or of the Last Supper. Extreme reformers did not approve of the new service because communicants were still expected to kneel, and they considered this to be idolatrous. Some historians attribute such objections to the Calvinism of Hooper and another extreme reformer, John Knox. It is also suggested that theirs was the influence behind the instructions sent to bishops to speed up the replacement of altars by communion tables, and to stop their clergy from wearing vestments when conducting services.

＊While these measures were being introduced, the government began a further attack on church wealth. In 1552 a survey of the temporal wealth of the bishops and all clergy with benefices worth more than £50 a year was undertaken. The resultant report estimated that these lands had a capital value of £1,087,000, and steps were taken to transfer some of this property to the Crown. The bishopric of Durham provides a typical example of this secularisation. Bishop Tunstall of Durham was arrested in October 1552 and imprisoned in the Tower of London. It was then proposed that his diocese should be divided into two parts. Durham itself was to be allocated £1,320 annually, and a new see of Newcastle was to be given an annual income of £665. This left an annual surplus of £2,000 from the income of the original bishopric, which was to be expropriated to the Crown. In the event this proposal never came into effect because of the death of Edward VI. At the same time commissioners had been sent out to draw up inventories and begin the removal of all the gold and silver plate still held by parish churches, and to list any items illegally removed since 1547. The commissioners had only just begun their work of confiscation when the King died and the operation was brought to an end, but not before some churches had lost their medieval plate (see page 86).

Some historians have seen this further attack on church wealth as yet another example of the greed of Northumberland. Others maintain that it was necessary if the Church of England was to be thoroughly reformed. Recently such actions have been interpreted as an expedient to improve royal finances after the bankruptcy resulting from the wars against France and Scotland. To Marxist historians it is clear evidence of the growing commercialism of the aristocracy and gentry, who were pressurising the government for a further redistribution of ecclesiastical wealth. Yet another explanation is that it was a political move to strengthen the control of the Church by the State. Without fresh evidence and research it is difficult to decide which one, or whichever combination of these explanations, is nearer the truth.

*What is certain is that the death of Edward VI and the fall of Northumberland brought this phase of the English Reformation to an abrupt end. The Forty-two Articles which had been drawn up to list the doctrines of the new Protestant Church of England never became law. All historians are agreed that by 1553 the Edwardian Reformation had resulted in a Church of England that was thoroughly Protestant. There is less unity over whether its doctrines were basically Lutheran, or to what extent they were influenced by Zwinglian, or Calvinist ideas. However, this is a matter of theological interpretation over which there is unlikely to be agreement. Yet historians do agree that, although the doctrines of the Church of England had been revolutionised, the political and administrative structure of the Church had remained unchanged. There is equal agreement that there is insufficient evidence at present to decide whether the people of England had wholeheartedly embraced the Protestant religion. Research at a local level has so far provided conflicting evidence. Although a majority of the landed élites and those in government circles seemed to favour moderate Protestantism, only a few of them did not find it possible to conform under Mary I. Many of the lower clergy and a majority of the population seem to have been largely indifferent to the religious debate. Only in London, the counties circling London and East Anglia does there appear to have been any widespread enthusiasm for the Protestant religion. Even there, a study of the county of Essex indicates more enthusiasm among the authorities in enforcing Protestantism, than among the general public in accepting it. At present historians do not agree with earlier interpretations which indicated wild enthusiasm for either Protestantism or Catholicism. They consider that Protestantism received general, if lukewarm, acceptance rather than widespread opposition.

5 The Marian Church 1553–8

While it is difficult to assess Northumberland's religious views, there is no doubt about those of Mary I. Some historians have described Mary as courageous, gentle and sympathetic. Others see her as being proud, arrogant, bigoted, narrow-minded and stupid. These views have not been greatly altered by recent research. However, all historians agree that she was passionately attached to the Roman Catholic religion. In 1553 no one in England doubted that Mary, after her 20 years of resistance to the royal supremacy for the sake of her religion, would restore Catholicism. There is good evidence to suggest that it was just as much Edward VI's wish to preserve Protestantism, as Northumberland's personal ambition, that led to the attempt to exclude Mary from the throne. Mary and her Catholic supporters saw the failure of the scheme as a miracle, and she was determined to restore England to the authority of Rome as quickly as possible. What Mary failed to realise was that her initial popularity sprang, not from a desire to see Catholicism restored, but from a dislike of Northumberland, and respect for the legitimate succession.

Her main supporters in England and abroad urged caution. Both Charles V and Pope Julius III warned her not to risk her throne by acting too rashly. Cardinal Reginald Pole, appointed as Papal Legate to restore England to the authority of Rome, stayed in the Netherlands for a year before coming to England. Whether this was because Charles V refused to allow the Cardinal to leave until the planned marriage between Philip and Mary had come to fruition, or whether it reflected Pole's natural caution about returning to his native land and a possibly hostile reception, is difficult to decide. Even Gardiner, Mary's most trusted English adviser, who had consistently resisted reform, was unenthusiastic about returning to papal authority. Mary singularly failed to realise the political implications of restoring Roman Catholicism to England. A return to papal authority would mean an end to the royal supremacy, which was strongly supported by the ruling and landed élites. Even the most ardent of the leading conservatives had been firm in their allegiance to the Crown and the Tudor State. Historians are agreed that the major causes of Mary's widespread unpopularity by the end of her reign, apart from the religious persecution, were the return to papal authority and the Spanish marriage, both of which were seen as interference by foreigners and an affront to English nationalism.

*However, in 1553 there was no doubt as to Mary's popularity, and the élites rallied to her support. The aristocracy and gentry were initially prepared to conform to Mary's religious views, and the bulk of the population followed their example. But some 800 strongly committed Protestants left the country and spent the remainder of the reign on the continent. Such an escape was less easy for the lower orders, and most of the 274 Protestant activists executed during Mary's reign came from this group. At the beginning of the reign even the most zealous of the urban radicals were not prepared to go against the mainstream of public opinion, and waited to see what would happen. Certainly, when Mary, using the royal prerogative, suspended the second Act of Uniformity and restored the mass, there was no public outcry.

This lack of religious opposition was apparent when Parliament met in October 1553. Admittedly, the arrest and imprisonment of Cranmer, Hooper and Ridley, along with other leading Protestant bishops, removed the major source of opposition in the House of Lords. After a lively, but not hostile debate, the first step towards removing all traces of Protestantism from the Church of England was achieved with the passing of the first Statute of Repeal. This Act swept away all the religious legislation approved by Parliament during the reign of Edward VI, and the doctrine of the Church of England was restored to what it had been in 1547 under the Act of the Six Articles.

The first Statute of Repeal, 1553
[Having repealed the Edwardian religious legislation.]

1 And be it further enacted by the authority aforesaid, that all such divine service and administration of Sacraments as were most commonly used in the realm of England in the last year of the reign of our late Sovereign Lord King Henry VIII shall be,
5 from and after the twentieth day of December in the present year of our Lord God 1553, used and frequented throughout the whole realm of England and all other the Queen's majesty dominions; and that no other kind nor order of divine service nor administration of sacraments be, after the said twentieth
10 day of December, used or ministered in any other manner, form or degree within the said realm of England, or other the Queen's dominions, that was most commonly used, ministered and frequented in the said last year of the reign of the said late King Henry VIII.

Although Mary had succeeded in re-establishing Catholicism, her advisers had managed to persuade her into some caution. There had been no attempt to question the royal supremacy, or to discuss the church lands which had been sold to the laity. Both these issues were likely to provoke a more heated debate.

Opposition to Mary's proposed marriage to Philip II of Spain and the consequent rebellion (see page 41), meant that further religious legislation was postponed until the spring of 1554. Gardiner, anxious to regain royal favour after his opposition to Mary's marriage (see page 40), tried to quicken the pace at which Protestantism was removed by persuading Parliament to pass a bill to re-introduce the heresy laws. He was successfully opposed by Paget, who feared that such a measure might provoke further disorder (see page 41). Thwarted in this direction, Gardiner proceeded to turn his attention to Protestant clergy. The Bishops of Gloucester, Hereford, Lincoln, Rochester and the Archbishop of York were deprived of their sees, and were replaced by committed Catholics. In March 1554 the bishops were instructed to enforce all the religious legislation of the last year of Henry VIII's reign. Apart from ensuring a return to 'the old order of the Church, in the Latin tongue', these injunctions demanded that all married clergy should give up their wives and families, or lose their livings. The authorities largely complied with these instructions, and some 800 parish clergy were so deprived. Although some fled abroad, the majority were found employment elsewhere in the country.

Cardinal Pole finally arrived in England in November 1554, and this marked the next decisive stage in the restoration of Roman Catholicism. Parliament met in the same month and passed the second Statute of Repeal. This Act ended the royal supremacy, and returned England to papal authority by repealing all the religious legislation of the reign of Henry VIII back to the time of the break with Rome. However, to achieve this Mary had to come to a compromise with the landed élites. Careful provision was made in the Act to protect the property rights of all those who had bought secularised church land since 1536. This demonstrates that Mary had to recognise the authority of Parliament over matters of religion. It meant that she had to forgo her plans for a full-scale restoration of the monasteries. Instead she had to be content with merely returning the monastic lands, worth £60,000 a year, still held by the Crown.

*At the same time Parliament approved the restoration of the old heresy laws. This marked the beginning of religious persecution. The first Protestant was burned at the stake for heresy on 4 February 1555, and Hooper suffered a similar fate five days later in his own city of Gloucester. In October Ridley and Hugh Latimer, the former bishop of Worcester, were likewise executed at Oxford, where they were followed by Cranmer in March 1556. The death of Gardiner in November 1555 had removed a trusted and restraining influence, and thereafter the regime became more repressive. Although Gardiner had started the persecution on the grounds that some executions would frighten the Protestant extremists into submission, he was too astute a politician to fail to see that the policy was not working. Far from cowing the Protestants, he realised that the executions were hardening the opposition to Mary and encouraging the colonies of English exiles on the continent. He counselled caution, but his advice was ignored. After his death, Mary, and Pole, who had been made Archbishop of Canterbury in December 1555, felt that it was their sacred duty to stamp out

The martyrdom of Cranmer in 1556, from Fox's Book of Martyrs

heresy, and stepped up the level of persecution. It is now estimated that the 274 religious executions carried out during the last three years of Mary's reign exceeded the number recorded in any Catholic country on the continent over the same period, even though it was much less than in some other periods. This modifies the claim by some historians that the Marian regime was more moderate than those on the continent.

Gardiner's unheeded warnings were soon justified, and Mary's popularity waned rapidly. There was widespread revulsion in the south-east of England against the persecution, and to many people Catholicism became firmly linked with dislike of Rome and Spain. Many local authorities either ignored, or tried to avoid enforcing, the unpopular legislation. The number of people fleeing abroad increased, reinforcing the colonies of English exiles living in centres of Lutheranism and Calvinism on the continent. They became the nucleus of an active and well-informed opposition, which began to flood England with anti-Catholic books and pamphlets. The effectiveness of this campaign is shown in the proclamations issued by the Privy Council in 1558, ordering the death penalty by martial law for anyone found with heretical or seditious literature. If before 1555 the English people were generally undecided about religion, the Marian repression succeeded in creating a core of highly committed English Protestants.

*Although Pole actively tried to eradicate Protestantism, his first priority appears to have been to restore stability after 20 years of religious turmoil. Historians consider that, in view of his lack of administrative experience and ability, such a formal and legalistic approach was a mistake. Indeed, a great part of Pole's three years in office were spent in the virtually hopeless task of trying to restore the Church of England's financial position. His attempts to reorganise and reconcile the Church of England to Rome were not helped by the death of Pope Julius III in 1555. The new Pope, Paul IV, disliked Pole and hated the Spanish Habsburgs. He stripped Pole of his title of Legate and ordered him to return to Rome. Pole refused to comply, and continued his work in England as Archbishop of Canterbury. However, this dispute, with its blatant papal intervention into English affairs, did little to convince anyone except the most zealous Catholics of the wisdom of returning to the authority of Rome.

Certainly such events did not help the government in its task of winning the hearts and minds of English men and women to the Catholic faith. Pole's hopes that, while he struggled with his administrative tasks, the re-establishment of the old religion would lead to wholehearted acceptance of Roman Catholicism were not to be realised. Pole was fully in favour of the educational programme which was being adopted on the continent and which, eventually, was to help the Counter Reformation to win back many converts there. He appointed capable and active bishops, all of whom subsequently refused to serve in the Elizabethan Protestant Church of England, and he established seminaries in every diocese for the training of priests. However, the majority of the parish clergy were still too uneducated, and displayed too little evangelical zeal, for this to have any immediate impact upon the laity. Mary's death in November 1558 came too soon for Catholic reform to have had any lasting effect. That is not to say that if Mary had lived longer, Catholicism would not have gained wider support than the significant minority, who clung to their faith after the establishment of the Elizabethan Church.

*To assess the state of religion in England in 1558 is just as difficult as it is to measure the advance of Protestantism by 1553. Historians are far from agreed as to what extent the bulk of the population had any particular leanings towards either the Protestant or the Catholic faiths. While it is easy to trace the changing pattern of official doctrine in the Church of England through the acts and statutes passed in Parliament, it is a much greater problem to determine what the general public thought about religion. At present the consensus among historians is that the ruling élites accepted the principle of the royal supremacy, and were prepared to conform to whichever form of religion was favoured by the monarch. Although the lower orders are considered generally to have had a conservative affection for the traditional forms of worship, it is thought they were prepared to follow the lead of the local élites.

Whether the religious legislation passed in Parliament was put into effect very much depended on the attitudes of the local élites, and to a lesser extent those of the parish authorities. For this reason historians have been carrying out detailed research into parish and county communities in the hope of revealing the religious attitudes among the laity. Such research uses the evidence of wills, parish registers, church wardens' accounts and court records to delve into local religious attitudes. Although such sources can be helpful they are often difficult to use. The following extract from the churchwardens' accounts for the parish of Stanford in the Vale illustrate some of these problems.

1 *1552* Item. in expences at Abingdon [a neighbouring town] going before the kings Comissioners about our church's goods.
Item. paid for a book of common prayer in English in the time of schism.
5 *1553* Item. in expences at Abingdon when the Church goods were carried to King Edward's comissioners.
Item. to the mason for setting up the high altar.
1554 Item. to Henry Snodnam gent for a table with a frame which served in the church for the communion in the wicked time of
10 schism.
Item. to Edythe Whayne for mending copes and vestments.
1556 Item. in expences to Abingdon of my lord Cardinal Pole's visitation.
Item. in expences to Abingdon to buy images.
15 Item. for writing a bill to answer certain Articles of Religion proposed by my lord Cardinal Pole to certain of the clergy and the Justices of the Peace to discuss.

These accounts show quite clearly that religious legislation was being enforced in the parish, but the problem is to decide what, if anything, this reveals about the attitudes of the local people. It might be assumed that, because the parish had complied with generally unpopular pieces of legislation for setting up communion tables and surrendering church plate, the parishioners were in favour of Protestantism. On the other hand, the speed with which the high altar was replaced in 1553 and the reference to Edward VI's reign as the wicked time of schism, might equally be interpreted as showing an attachment to Catholicism. In any case the record of religious changes might merely indicate that the local authorities were conforming to government policy, and show nothing about popular attitudes. This is very much the difficulty encountered in local studies. Lancashire élites are shown to have actively resisted the introduction of reformed religion, while in Essex Protestantism is seen to have been enthusiastically enforced. In neither case is much revealed about the views of the general public. Nor are historians confident that the findings for one county are typical for the local region, far less for the whole country. One recent study, based on Devon and Cornwall, does seem to have succeeded in finding out more about popular attitudes. This is an area where, because of the Western Rebellion, historians expected to find strong religious conservatism. However, the study, while revealing no zeal for Protestantism, uncovered equally little enthusiasm for Catholicism. Indeed, by 1558 passivity and indifference seem to have replaced religious fervour in the West Country.

In general it appears that by 1558 the majority of people in England were still undecided about religion. Among the élites there was strong support for the royal supremacy, but they were willing to follow the

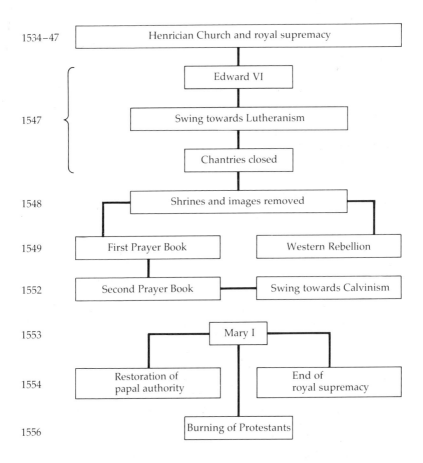

Summary – Religious Change 1547–58

religion of the legitimate monarch. The mass of the population do not appear to have had strong formalised convictions, and in most cases they were prepared to follow the lead of their social superiors. Although there were small minorities of committed Protestants and Catholics, neither religion seems to have had a strong hold in England when Mary I died. When Elizabeth I came to the throne the country was willing to return to a form of moderate Protestantism. However, during her reign deeper religious divisions began to appear, and the unity of the Church of England came to an end.

Making notes on 'Religious Change 1547–58'

You need to remember that religion was a major issue in mid-Tudor England, and that it interlocked with every other aspect of life. Your notes should not just help you to answer questions specifically on religion, but should also indicate where religion played an important part in politics, foreign policy, and social and economic change. There is still much debate among historians as to whether Protestantism was gaining, or Catholicism retaining, the loyalty of the general public. Religion is a controversial topic and the thinking about its role in mid-Tudor England is still very provisional. It is important that your notes are organised to give you a clear grasp of the sequence of religious changes, but they must also indicate the wider implications at each stage. The following headings, sub-headings and questions should help you:

1.   Introduction.
1.1. How have the views of historians about religious changes between 1547 and 1558 altered in recent years?
1.2. To what extent was religion an important political issue?
1.3. How did religious considerations affect foreign policy?
2.   The Henrician Church in 1547.
2.1. In what ways had the religious balance in the Henrician Church changed between 1534 and 1547?
2.2. What were the main elements of Catholic faith retained in the English Church by 1547?
2.3. What Protestant practices had already been adopted by the English Church by 1547?
3.   The Edwardian Church 1547–9.
3.1. What were the attitudes of Somerset, the Privy Council and the bishops towards religious reform?
3.2. What were the religious views of the people outside the ruling circles?
3.3. What were the first moves towards religious reform? Why did

these not satisfy the more active reformers? Why did they provoke protest among both Catholics and Protestants?

3.4. What measures of religious reform were introduced by Parliament in November 1547, and what were the consequences?

3.5. What changes were introduced by the first Act of Uniformity in 1549, and how popular were they with the laity?

3.6. What were the causes, course and outcome of the Western Rebellion?

3.7. What religious views were expressed by the rebels, and what was the attitude of the government towards their demands?

4. The Edwardian Church 1550–3.

4.1. How did Northumberland clear the way for religious reform?

4.2. What reforms were introduced, and how were they received?

4.3. What measures were taken in 1551 to prepare for more reform?

4.4. What further religious reforms were introduced in 1552?

4.5. How Protestant was the Church of England by 1553?

5. The Marian Church 1553–8.

5.1. What did Mary see as her religious duty?

5.2. What form of religion was restored by Mary? What was not restored?

5.3. Why did religious persecution begin in 1555? What were the effects of the persecution of Protestants?

5.4. Why did Archbishop Pole find it difficult to rekindle enthusiasm for the Catholic faith?

5.5. Why do historians find it difficult to assess the views of the laity about the mid-century changes in religion?

Answering essay questions on 'Religious Change 1547–58'

Questions on mid-Tudor religion are likely to extend beyond the period covered by this book. It is, therefore, essential that you attempt to form a coherent view of the changes that took place in religion in England from about 1530 to about 1560. Consider the following questions (pay particular attention to the timescales covered by each question):

1. 'Why was there so little popular opposition to the Henrician and Edwardian Reformations?'

2. 'How far were the religious changes of the 1550s in England the result of public pressure?'

3. 'To what extent was the Edwardian Reformation Protestant?'

4. 'What were the consequences for England of Edward and Mary's personal religious beliefs?'

Question 1 is of the straightforward 'why?' variety, and can be answered by a series of 'because' points. Make a list of all the 'because' answers you could use in this question. If you end up with a large number of overlapping answers, group similar ones together to make four or five major points. These might include 'general religious apathy', 'widespread deference to authority' and 'the growth of nationalism'. What criteria would you use to decide the order in which to present your points?

Questions 2 and 3 are of the same general type. What should be the two main parts of answers to such questions? Make a list of the evidence you would need to consider in answering question 3. Plan an answer to this question, including paragraphs on doctrine, organisation and practices in each half.

Source-based questions on 'Religious Change 1547–58'

1   The First Edwardian Act of Uniformity, 1549
Read the extract from the First Edwardian Act of Uniformity, given on page 73, and answer the following questions:
a) Which previous Act was replaced by this legislation? (1 mark)
b) Who was the Archbishop of Canterbury, referred to in line 1? (1 mark)
c) What were the implications of the words 'to the most sincere and pure Christian religion taught by the Scripture, as to usages of the primitive Church' (lines 5–6)? (6 marks)
d) Why was the government anxious to introduce a uniform order of worship? (2 marks)

2   The articles of the Western Rebels, 1549
Read the extract from the articles of the Western Rebels, given on pages 75–6, and answer the following questions:
a) Were the rebels demanding a return to Catholicism or an extension of Protestantism? (1 mark)
b) What was the 'new service' referred to in line 18? (1 mark)
c) What were the implications of article X (lines 20–1)? (5 marks)
d) Which phrase in another article is making a similar demand to article X? (1 mark)
e) What was it about the form (as opposed to the content) of the articles that particularly antagonised the Privy Council? (2 marks)

3   The first Statute of Repeal, 1553
Read the extract from the first Statute of Repeal, given on page 82, and answer the following questions:
a) Why did Mary need an Act of Parliament in order to return the country to Catholic doctrine and forms of worship? (3 marks)

b) What was being reversed by the Act? (2 marks)

c) In what ways was the Act not a complete restoration of Catholicism? (5 marks)

4 Religious change at a local level, 1552–6

Study the extract from the churchwardens' accounts, given on page 86, and answer the following questions:

a) Which Act of Parliament required parishes to purchase an English prayer book? How long had it taken the churchwardens of Stanford to comply with the new law? What can be deduced from this? (5 marks)

b) What 'Church goods' are being referred to in line 5? Why were they being taken to the King's commissioners? (4 marks)

c) What can be deduced from the use of the phrase 'in the wicked time of schism' (lines 9–10)? (3 marks)

d) In what ways had the religious changes of the period 1552–6 imposed additional costs on the parish of Stanford? (3 marks)

5 The death-bed of Henry VIII

Study the painting of the death-bed of Henry VIII reproduced on page 72. Answer the following questions:

a) Why is Henry VIII shown pointing to Edward? (1 mark)

b) The painting was produced in 1548 for propaganda purposes. Explain in detail the propaganda points that the artist is attempting to make. (7 marks)

c) How far does the painting constitute reliable evidence about what happened at Henry VIII's death-bed? (2 marks)

CHAPTER 5

A Crisis in Society?

1 Introduction

Historians agree that the sixteenth century was a highly significant period when major changes were taking place within English society. However, because social change is such a slow, long-term process, it is virtually impossible to measure it over short periods of time such as between 1547 and 1558. Instead historians have to try to assess what stage the series of complicated structural changes which had begun in the fourteenth century (see page 9) had reached by the middle of the sixteenth century. At the same time they have to consider what effects, if any, particular events such as the Reformation were having upon society. Only then is it possible to reach any conclusions about whether there was a mid-century social crisis, or the extent to which social change contributed to any of the problems facing Tudor governments at that time.

It is widely agreed that by the middle of the sixteenth century, although the actual shape of the social structure had not altered, the changes that were taking place were causing stresses within the fabric of society. However, the extent to which any such tensions contributed to the popular unrest in 1549 is not clear. This uncertainty reflects the lack of agreement among historians as to the nature of the changes taking place. Marxist historians maintain that the social changes taking place were mainly the consequence of shifts in economic relationships at all levels. Revisionist historians, on the other hand, consider that changes in political relationships among the élites were the major influence on the social structure. However, many historians are not convinced by either of these two major explanations of social change. They stress the importance of religious change, the variations in population levels, and the effect of inflation in creating movements within and between social groups.

* There is considerable disagreement among Marxist historians over the explanation of the emergence of what they see as an increasingly capitalistic society during the first half of the sixteenth century. The most orthodox theory is that there was a complete change in agricultural relationships. This is seen as starting during the feudal crisis, which had been caused by a breakdown in relations between landlords and peasant farmers. During the fifteenth century the English peasant communities had been strong enough to free themselves from labour services and other feudal dues, so that they had much greater control over their land and paid lower rents. In the sixteenth century the landlords were able to use their political power to push up the level of rents, and so begin to force the peasants off their land. Former peasant

smallholdings were consolidated into larger farms, which were either leased out or kept by the landowner. In both cases the land was farmed commercially, using the now landless, former peasantry as labour. This, it is maintained, created a new, exploitive capitalistic relationship between landholders and landless labourers. Marxist historians consider it to have been this loss of independence that led to resentment and class conflict between wage labourers and landowners.

Other Marxist historians offer different explanations for the emergence of a capitalistic society. One of the main alternative suggestions has been that the growth of world trade made labour relationships based on market forces more attractive to both landlords and peasants than the old feudal ones. Estate owners found it more profitable to produce food for sale, and to work their land by wage labour. Some peasant smallholders either used the situation to acquire more land and become yeomen, selling food for the market, or to give up their land altogether to work for wages. However, many peasants preferred to retain their smallholdings and to remain self-sufficient. It was this that caused tensions between a self-sufficient peasant economy and market forces. At the same time it created class conflict between the peasant smallholders and the new commercial farmers.

Other Marxist historians attach more importance to the spread of urban and industrial relationships, already based on wage labour, into the countryside. They see this as an essential step towards a capitalistic society. Since the thirteenth century merchants and industrialists had been transferring some of the textile trades from the towns into the countryside, where they could employ cheaper peasant labour. This is seen as creating tensions between urban and rural communities. At the same time they were buying country estates and introducing more commercial techniques using wage labour. These methods were adopted by many of their rural neighbours, and so commercial farming spread, particularly near towns. This growing commercial group created a new class, the 'bourgeoisie'. The Crown is seen as favouring the bourgeoisie because it could use its members to staff the growing state bureaucracy, and so reduce the influence of the aristocracy. This, it is maintained, created class conflict between the bourgeoisie and the aristocracy, which the Crown used to strengthen its own position. At the same time there is seen to be growing class conflict between the expanding industrial labour force and its employers.

These various Marxist theories of social change see the emergence of capitalistic relationships causing class conflict at all levels within English society. This was once thought to be the major cause of the widespread popular discontent in the middle of the sixteenth century, which led to peasant rebellions in 1549. However, many historians, even Marxists, are now very doubtful whether there is any evidence of class, let alone class conflict in the sixteenth century.

*Revisionist historians, while agreeing that it started with the feudal crisis, offer an entirely different explanation of social change. For them, social restructuring was caused by shifts in political relationships among the landed and ruling élites caused by the rise of the State. The feudal anarchy caused by quarrels among the aristocracy had enabled western European monarchs to gain greater authority through the support of the bulk of the population. This meant that the State was able to centralise political power, and reduce the influence of the aristocracy in the provinces. Consequently, it is maintained, the aristocracy and the other landed élites became dependent upon the State for support. To maintain their social, political and economic position they had to rely upon royal patronage to give them offices at Court, in the government or in the army. Revisionist historians see the social changes developing in England during the first half of the sixteenth century in terms of an élitist power struggle. For them, it was their success in obtaining offices from the Crown that led to the rise of the gentry. Revisionist historians totally disagree with Marxist and other historians who maintain that the gentry rose because of their ability to exploit the favourable economic conditions of the early part of the sixteenth century. They see the emergence of men like Somerset and Northumberland resulting entirely from their success in obtaining royal favour, at the expense of established aristocratic families such as the Howards, the Dukes of Norfolk. The fall of Somerset in 1549, and the ensuing rivalry between the conservatives and the reformers, can be interpreted as part of the élite power struggle.

Many historians are not convinced by this revisionist explanation of social change. They consider that the so-called power struggle was just part of the normal rise and fall of aristocratic and gentry families, and they can see no evidence that the early Tudors favoured new families in preference to the ancient aristocracy. It has also been pointed out that this theory has the great weakness that it does not account for social change among the rest of the population.

*Some historians see the Reformation as being particularly important in the process of social change. It is considered that the break from Rome and the introduction of Protestantism (see page 66) was essential to promote the spread of individualism, capitalism and competition. This, it is suggested, is why many of the élites and commercial groups adopted moderate Protestantism, so that they could benefit from the growth of market forces. Equally the seizure of church lands is seen as helping the élites to build up their wealth, and to recover from the economic problems caused by the feudal crisis. It is claimed that the Western Rebellion of 1549 (see page 75) provides evidence of such developments. Certainly the rebels were hostile towards the local gentry, who, they claimed, were using the Reformation to enrich themselves. At the same time, the adoption of Lutheran and Calvinist ideas during the reign of Edward VI is seen as introducing the Protestant work ethic into England, with its stress on thrift, sobriety and hard work. This, along with the attack upon superstitious rituals and Holy Days, is considered to have begun to break down the seasonal life of the peasantry. It was the threat to their lifestyle as much as their attachment to the Catholic religion, it is thought, that provoked the rebels in the West Country in 1549. Although some historians are doubtful about the long-term effect of religion on social change because of the apparent apathy of the majority of the population, there is no doubt about its immediate impact between 1547 and 1553.

*Many social and economic historians are not completely convinced by any of these general theories of social change. They consider that variations in the levels of population and the consequent inflation, or deflation, had a major influence on the social structure. For them the deflationary period following the Black Death of 1349 created a period of peasant prosperity, and caused economic problems for the landed élites (see page 10). When the population began to recover at the beginning of the sixteenth century the situation was reversed. Landowners now began to benefit from increased prices caused by inflation. At the same time they were able to push up rents because more people were looking for land to rent. This in turn is seen as forcing many peasants from the land because they could not afford the higher rents. As more people were available for work, wages did not increase at the same rate as prices. Consequently the living standards of both peasant and wage labourer are seen to have been falling, while most of the élites were prospering. It is thought that the effect of this change was being fully felt by 1549, and was a cause of the popular unrest.

*Thus, there is a wide disparity of views among historians as to both the cause of social change, and its possible impact by the middle of the sixteenth century. Although all the various theories suggest that there were social tensions in mid-Tudor England, it is doubtful whether they amounted to a social crisis. Indeed, it can be maintained that popular discontent was always close to the surface in pre-industrial societies where so many people lived close to the poverty line. Only in times of acute hardship, such as famine or widespread unemployment, did grievances erupt into violence. So it might well be said that the mid-century problems were the result of an economic crisis more than a social one (see Chapter 6).

2 Social Mobility and the Social Structure

Although general theories of social change are useful to indicate what might have been happening to society over long periods of time, they are not very helpful in showing the actual structure of society at any particular moment. It is just as difficult to find out in detail how society was changing in the middle of the sixteenth century, as it is to decide what the general public really thought about religion. The reason for this is the lack of reliable evidence. From the time of the Domesday

Book of 1086 until the 1801 census, no English government had thought it necessary to carry out a detailed survey of the numbers and occupations of the population. For the period in between these two dates, historians have to rely upon the evidence of such things as parish registers, taxation lists, local surveys, wills and inventories, household accounts or contemporary writings to try to build up a picture of society. Apart from their potential unreliability, such sources are very fragmentary and so it is possible to obtain only occasional glimpses of what was happening. In any case the rate of social development varied in different parts of the country. For this reason it is unwise to assume that just because certain changes were taking place in Kent, the same thing was happening in Yorkshire. Consequently careful comparisons have to be made between local studies before any general conclusions can be drawn. To overcome these difficulties, historians create social models in order to be able to measure change and continuity over time. However, it must be remembered that such models only create a very simplified picture of society, and ignore many of the underlying complexities.

*Historians agree that English society underwent an important period of evolution between 1350 and 1550. Mid-sixteenth-century society is seen as being more competitive and individualistic than it had been during the Middle Ages. Even so, it is considered that it was still overwhelmingly rural, and retained many of the characteristics of feudal society (see page 14). To measure the nature and extent of the changes taking place over these 200 years historians construct models of late feudal and early Tudor society. One of the most important signs of change is thought to be the amount of social mobility existing between the various groups. Therefore it is important to understand the nature of the social mobility which existed in late medieval society.

The late medieval social model is seen as being a pyramid of status based on land ownership, which contained 95 per cent of the population. At the top was the king, who was the main landowner. Below him came the nobility (dukes, marquises, earls, viscounts and barons), which was made up of some 60 families. These great estate owners, along with their wives and families, formed the top rank of society. A nobleman's position within the aristocratic élite depended upon the amount of land he possessed. Smaller landowners, consisting of younger sons and new entrants, formed a second tier below the nobility. Under them came the yeomen, who had to own land worth at least 40 shillings a year. At the bottom was the great bulk of the population, the peasantry, who rented smallholdings on the manors of the élites. The remaining five per cent of the population consisted of the clergy and town dwellers. The clerical hierarchy depended not on birth and size of estates, but on the importance of the position held. At the top was the Archbishop of Canterbury with the parish clergy at the bottom. Towns are seen as being outside the rural feudal structure, with populations that were more individualistic and educated than that of the surrounding countryside. Status in the urban hierarchy was based on wealth, and at the top were rich merchants and the master craftsmen of the guilds. Below them came the shopkeepers, small traders, journeymen and apprentices. The great mass of town society was made up of servants, labourers and the poor.

* Social mobility, although limited, is seen as taking place within and between these three hierarchies. Members of the aristocratic élite were socially equal to each other and the king. Apart from the hereditary nobility the only other title among the group was that of knight. This was a military distinction, and theoretically was only granted by the king, a feudal superior, or a military commander on the battlefield as a mark of bravery. Educational opportunities were limited. Boys were given a military training, and the girls were taught the art of household management. Successful marriage alliances were seen as a major means of upward social mobility. Daughters were frequently married off very early (although not before the age of seven) to secure military, political or financial alliances. Only the eldest son could inherit the family estates, so younger sons had to seek alternative careers. A minority entered the Church or one of the monastic orders, where they could achieve high office either in England or on the continent. As the clergy were the only educated section of society, successful clerics often obtained important offices in the royal government. A religious career in one of the orders of nuns also offered an alternative to marriage for the daughters of the élites. War was the predominant interest of the élites. Family fortunes could be recouped, and penniless younger sons could start their careers from the ransoms, booty and glory to be won in a successful military campaign.

For the remainder of rural society, social mobility was much more limited. Among the yeomen there was a certain amount of upward mobility into the lower ranks of the élites through success in farming, trade, industry, war or marriage. However, the great majority of the peasantry were not free. Legally they were serfs, and were the property of the landowner on whose manor they lived. This meant that they were not allowed to leave without the permission of the lord of the manor, and so there was little opportunity for either social or geographical mobility. As in the case of the élites it was normally only the eldest son who could inherit the family smallholding. Younger children frequently stayed at home and helped on the farm until a vacant holding became available, and they could get married. This meant that most of the rural population lived and died within a few miles of where they were born. A few fortunate younger children, whose parents had enough money to buy permission for them to leave the manor, were able to gain upward social mobility. Some went into the Church or monastic orders, while others became apprenticed in one of the craft industries in the towns.

Urban societies, with the exception of London, were small and inward looking. Strong commercial rivalry meant that outsiders were regarded with suspicion, and so found it difficult to establish themselves. As only the eldest son inherited the family business, even younger children found it very difficult to break into the close-knit ruling circles. However, like the Church, towns offered a means of social mobility within an otherwise stable rural hierarchy. For the lower orders the towns provided some opportunity for geographical mobility, and the chance of improved social status for the lucky few. Only for those in, or reaching, the town ruling circles was considerable social mobility possible. Wealthy merchants were able to buy country estates and merge into the landed élites, or to marry their sons and daughters into noble or aristocratic families.

3 Early Tudor Society

The events taking place in the late fourteenth and fifteenth centuries, however interpreted, are seen as causing a quickening in the pace of social change. However, although it is agreed that significant changes were taking place within society, it is thought that its actual structure remained the same. The three social hierarchies stayed broadly unaltered in size and their relationship to each other. The feudal crisis is seen as affecting both the towns and the Church in economic terms, but having no impact upon their social structure. It was rural society that is considered to have been changed both economically and socially.

The great landowners, both lay and ecclesiastical, are considered to have lost economic and political power to the Crown. In addition, the nobility forfeited their military independence. The social effect of this change was to make the king the social superior of the élites, instead of their equal. Under the early Tudors such superiority was reinforced by the concept of the monarch being the father of the nation to whom all subjects owed obedience (see page 6). Another consequence of the economic decline of the great landowners was that during the fifteenth century some of them had to sell part of their land, and lease out much of the remainder on long leases of up to 99 years. The immediate impact of this was the temporary lowering of the social prestige of the nobility. They could no longer afford to maintain their great households, and service to the Crown became more attractive to the ambitious among the lesser élites. Likewise, the sale and leasing out of the great estates created a very active land market, which widened the availability of land. This was the beginning of the rise of the gentry. The old élite became divided into two parts. Aristocratic society – the nobles and their immediate families – assumed the rank below the monarch. Their younger children, their families and their descendants evolved into a lesser élite – the gentry – below the aristocracy. There were three ranks in this new social group. At the top were the knights. The title had partially lost its old military significance, although it still was not hereditary. Knights could be created for a variety of reasons, yet the title increasingly came to denote a landowner with estates worth at least £100 a year. Next in rank to the knight was the esquire – a title given to the children of knights and their descendants. The lowest rank among the gentry was the gentleman – a title given to the younger children of esquires and their descendants.

All the existing means of social mobility remained the same. The major change was that there had been a significant redistribution of land to the new gentry. When prices and rents began to rise after 1500 it was the gentry who benefited from such increases, and from the improving industrial and commercial conditions. The aristocracy were unable to reap any real profit from their estates until the long leases ran out towards the end of the sixteenth century and they were able to repossess their land.

The impact of the feudal crisis on the lower orders is seen as bringing equally significant social consequences. The decline in economic and political power among the great landowners is considered to have brought about the disappearance of serfdom and labour services in England during the fifteenth century. All the peasantry were now theoretically free (although there were still serfs in some parts of England until the end of the sixteenth century), and so could move about the country as they chose. This is seen as altering the structure of peasant society. Peasant smallholders were generally described as husbandmen. Customary tenures were being replaced by a new form of tenancy for the lifetime of the holder called copyhold, for which rent was paid in cash. Many of the former peasants took advantage of the availability of land and amassed holdings of up to 200 acres. They became commercial farmers, and joined the ranks of the yeomen. Now that the new copyhold tenancies no longer carried the stigma of being unfree, many of the former yeomen and new gentry were also prepared to acquire this type of land. However, many peasant husbandmen preferred to remain self-sufficient smallholders, with about 30–40 acres of land. At the same time some improved their position by acquiring enough land to become self-sufficient. Others preferred to continue to supplement the produce of their smallholdings by working for wages on the commercial farms and in rural industry. A significant number decided to take advantage of the higher wage levels created by the fall in the size of the labour force, and abandon their land to work full-time for wages. All the existing routes of social mobility remained the same, but, because the lower orders now enjoyed much greater geographical mobility, many more people could take advantage of them.

*Another highly significant development which is considered to have altered the pattern of social mobility, particularly among the élites, was the spread of the Renaissance and Christian humanism in England at the end of the fifteenth century. These Renaissance ideas are seen as weakening the influence of the Church. Apart from causing a growth in anti-clericalism by attacking the wealth and abuses in the Church, Renaissance thought encouraged the spread of secular education. Previously a clerical career was seen as not just an opportunity to obtain high office in the Church, but as a means of gaining important governmental positions. The spread of Christian humanism, with its emphasis on education for the laity, promoted the universities, the legal Inns of Court and secular schools as an alternative for political careerists. Thomas Wolsey, the son of a Suffolk cattle dealer who rose to become a cardinal, the Archbishop of York, and Lord Chancellor under Henry VIII, is seen as the last of the great English clerical careerists. His successors, such as Thomas Cromwell and William Cecil, came to power through a university and legal education. Increasingly this became the route taken by those aspiring to a political and administrative career.

*The difficulty facing historians is to decide how quickly such changes were taking place. Fortunately a remarkably full picture of English society is provided in 1522. In that year the Privy Council ordered a survey to be made of all men fit for military service. At the same time the government used the survey to inquire into the value of land and movable goods held by everyone in the country in order to draw up new tax schedules. As a result the survey provides the most comprehensive census of English society between 1086 and 1801. Unfortunately the muster returns for 1522 have only survived for a number of counties. However, over the past 20 years historians have used them to analyse the state of early Tudor society.

The picture that emerges from the muster returns is of considerable underlying continuity, but there are clear signs that early capitalist society was becoming established by the 1520s. England was still predominantly rural, and most of the population still lived in small villages. The Church continued to be the largest single holder of land, and there is little evidence of any marked changes in the composition of urban society. However, although the villages were mainly made up of communities of husbandmen, most of them had at least one (and usually more) commercial farmer, or yeoman. It is also clear that the number of servants and labourers had increased noticeably, and it is estimated that 40 per cent of the lower orders were wage-earners. The rise of the gentry was clearly well advanced. By the 1520s they held some 30 per cent of the manors, and were the leaseholders of many more.

Shellingford was a small village in Berkshire and shows many of the characteristics of a rural community in the 1520s. The local abbey still owned the manor. There are two small pieces of freehold land, one held by a member of the local gentry, the other by a husbandman from the nearby village of Stanford. The parson held a large piece of land attached to the parsonage. What is not shown is that Thomas Unton's brother Alexander Unton, gentleman, had held the lease of the manor

The Muster Certificate for Shellingford, 1522

1 *The value of lands & property there*
The Abbot of Abingdon is chief lord there & his lands are in
value by the year over all charges   £40 0s 0d
Thomas Unton Gent. in lands   6s 8d
5 John Elyotte in lands   5s 8d
Sir William Craddock Clerk is parson there & his parsonage is
in value by the year over all charges   £13 0s 0d

The value of goods & other movable property there

John Wyse senior householder	£22 0s 0d
10 John White servant	12s 0d
John Yate h.	£5 0s 0d
Robert Barteley servant	£1 0s 0d
Thomas Abday h.	£7 0s 0d
Thomas Seuernake	£2 0s 0d
15 John Bowell h.	£4 0s 0d
William Badnoll h.	£13 6s 8d
Robert Ryve servant	£1 6s 8d
Thomas Carter servant	£1 0s 0d
William Browne h.	£1 0s 0d
20 John Cowley h.	£2 0s 0d
John Chirchey h.	£3 0s 0d
John Tayllor h.	£12 0s 0d
William Yate h.	£14 0s 0d
Thomas Yate his son	£2 0s 0d
25 William Somner servant	10s 0d
Harry Harne h.	£1 0s 0d
Phillippe Smythe h.	£2 0s 0d
John Smythe h.	£5 6s 8d
Margory Chirche widow	£1 0s 0d
30 Julyan Chirche widow	£1 0s 0d
Margett of Acris widow	10s 0d

from the abbey for 33 years from 1508. None of these people lived in
the village; the residents are listed under the goods and property
valuation. All of them marked householder or with 'h.' were the head of
a farm or smallholding. It has been estimated that in 1522 anyone with
goods worth more than nine pounds was a yeoman, and that any
husbandman with goods worth between five pounds and nine pounds
was self-sufficient. Clearly by 1522 there was already a wide disparity in
wealth between the villagers.

Although historians have succeeded in constructing a reasonably clear picture of the shape of English society in the 1520s, lack of evidence makes it much more difficult to decide how far it had developed by the middle of the century. There seems to be little evidence that the increase in population had begun to affect the living standards of the lower orders by the 1520s. There were still copyholds available at a reasonable rent, and prices had not risen sufficiently to outstrip wages in a significant way. However, it is considered that the buoyant land market of the fifteenth century was beginning to become static, and that demand for land among the élites had begun to exceed the supply. There is seen to be growing rivalry between the aristocracy, gentry and yeomen for land. Such competition was not caused just by the increased numbers of gentry and yeomen. By the 1520s commercial opportunities were improving for landowners. Many of the great estate owners, whose land was still tied up with long leases, wished to obtain additional land so that they could take advantage of the upturn in the economy. In addition, leaseholders were anxious to convert their leases into freehold, or to obtain other land, before the term of their tenancy ran out. Historians see this situation as potentially dangerous for the Crown, as it was causing instability among the élites.

   *Some historians consider that there is a clear link between this situation and the English Reformation. They suggest that Henry VIII embarked on the spoliation of the English Church in order to satisfy the growing land hunger among the élites. Clearly it was in the interests of both the parties to subordinate the Church to the secular powers. In addition it was vital to the Crown that it should keep the active support of the élites. To maintain this claim it is pointed out that both reformers and conservatives among the élites were firm supporters of the royal supremacy. Furthermore it is indicated that Catholics were just as active in acquiring church property as were the Protestants. Such an interpretation, it is claimed, is confirmed by the complete solidarity among the Protestant and Catholic élites in resisting Mary I's attempts in 1554 to restore all church lands sold after 1536. On the other hand, it can just as convincingly be argued that the élites were simply taking advantage of the availability of land that came as a result of the Reformation.

   Whichever of the many explanations of the English Reformation is accepted, the result was that by 1553, church lands with an annual value of some five million pounds had passed into lay ownership. This was the largest redistribution of land since the Norman Conquest and was, clearly, to have a considerable impact on the structure of élite society. Marxist historians, in particular, see the Reformation as a vital stage in the development of capitalist society in England. However, this is a long-term view, and the immediate consequences on mid-Tudor society are not apparent. In north Berkshire in 1536 the Church held 51 per cent of the freehold land, 33 per cent of which belonged to the monasteries. Of the remainder the gentry held 34 per cent, the King 8 per cent and the aristocracy 7 per cent. By 1553 the gentry held 51 per cent, while the Crown and the aristocracy had both increased their share slightly. Such figures vary from county to county, but it is clear that the gentry were the major beneficiaries of the sale of monastic land. However, it must be remembered that in many cases the gentry were already the leasees of the estates that they purchased. For example, the manor of Shellingford (see page 101) was surrendered to the Crown by Abingdon Abbey in 1538. In 1539 the King granted the estate to the leasee, Alexander Unton, at a ground rent of £4.13s.4d per year. He also bought the neighbouring royal manor of Hatford in 1544. The immediate effect of the sale of church land seems to have been that the existing gentry consolidated their position by converting leaseholds into permanent possession, or by acquiring additional estates. The same applies to the nobility, who added church land to their already considerable territorial holdings. By 1558 only a small amount of land appears to have passed into the possession of new owners from the towns or industry. However, there is plenty of evidence to show that in the Home Counties, particularly in Kent, London merchants were very active in the land market even at this stage.

It appears that by 1558 the secularisation of ecclesiastical property had had very little effect on the structure of élite society. With the exception of the immediate vicinity of London, the land had gone to consolidate the position of the existing aristocracy and gentry. The Church had lost a great deal of wealth and power. In due course this was to lower the prestige of the clergy and make a clerical career less attractive to the younger sons of the élites, but this was not apparent in 1558. It is true that the opportunity for a monastic career in England had vanished, but with a buoyant land market and a growing variety of other career opportunities, it is doubtful that this was regarded by the élites as a serious loss. However, while other career routes for younger sons remained the same, for daughters, the disappearance of the nunneries left marriage as the only possible opening.

For the remainder of society the redistribution of land had little, or no, immediate effect. The losses sustained by the Church left the clerical hierarchy unchanged, apart from the disappearance of abbots, which lessened ecclesiastical influence in the House of Lords. Similarly the urban hierarchies remained unaltered. Some of the town élites enhanced their position by purchasing blocks of ecclesiastical urban property, while a few had succeeded in moving into the ranks of the gentry through buying a country estate. This provided some openings for new entrants into the town ruling bodies, but otherwise the opportunities for upward social mobility remained the same. For the great majority – the rural and urban non-élites – the redistribution of land had no effect whatsoever. All that happened was that they became the tenants of new landowners. In the past it has been suggested that the new owners were more rapacious than the old ecclesiastical landlords. This view has now been rejected. It is considered that church-owned land and property had been just as vigorously exploited as that held by the laity. In any case, as many of the church estates passed into the ownership of former leasees, it is unlikely that there was any noticeable change in management.

*By 1558 it appears that there had been little further change to the social structure at any level. Changes to élite society resulting from the feudal crisis had progressed and been consolidated. The monarchy had established its position of social and political superiority. By recouping their economic losses the nobility and aristocracy had consolidated themselves as the major landowning group below the King. The gentry had risen, and become established as the rank immediately below the aristocracy. Yeomen were recognised as the major farmers below the gentry. The urban and clerical hierarchies remained unchanged. Self-sufficient husbandmen were still the most numerous group in the rural communities. The number of wage-earners had increased and they were forming a growing rural and urban proletariat.

At this point it must be asked whether historians are justified in making such a reconstruction of the early capitalist English social hierarchy. For this purpose it is necessary to compare their social model with a contemporary view of mid-Tudor society. In 1565 Sir Thomas Smith, who had been Secretary of State under Somerset, wrote the book *The Commonwealth of England* (*De Republica Anglorum*), in which he described English society as he saw it. It must be remembered that this was an élite viewpoint, and it is not possible to be sure of the author's motives for writing the book. It may be that he was depicting society as he thought it should be, rather than showing it as it actually existed in the middle of the sixteenth century. Again he might, like the Norfolk rebels (see page 112), be nostalgically looking back to a society which he thought was vanishing.

1 Of the first part of Gentlemen of England, called *nobilitas major*.
   . . . In England no man is created baron, except he may dispend of yearly revenue one thousand pounds . . .
   Of the second sort of Gentlemen, which may be called *nobilitas*
5 *minor* . . . No man is a knight by succession, not the king or prince . . . knights therefore be not born but made . . .
   Esquires be all those which bear arms . . . these be taken for no distinct order of the commonwealth, but do go with the residue of gentlemen . . . Gentlemen be those whom their blood and race
10 doth make noble and known . . . For whosoever studieth the laws of the realm, who studieth in the Universities . . . and to be short, who can live idly and without manual labour, and will bear the port, charge and countenance of a gentleman, he shall be called master . . .
15 Those whom we call yeomen, next unto the nobility, knights and

squires . . . is a freeman born English, and may dispend of his
own free land in yearly revenue to the sum of 40s. sterling . . .
The fourth sort or class amongst us, is of those . . . day labourers,
poor husbandmen, yea merchants or retailers which have no free
20 land, copyholders and all artificers [wage labourers] . . . These
have no voice nor authority in our commonwealth, and no
account is made of them, but only to be ruled.

4 A Social Crisis 1547–58?

In the past a number of historians have concluded that the popular
rebellions and the élite power struggle in 1549 indicate a social crisis at
all levels of society. In view of the apparent stability in all the social
hierarchies this view is no longer widely held. In social terms neither
the urban, nor the clerical hierarchies displayed any signs of pressure.
Furthermore, no drastic change can be seen in the pattern of social
development among the lower orders. After 200 years of transition
English society appears to have reached a firm platform, which was to
act as a springboard for the next phase of transformation.

A number of suggestions have been put forward to support the
contention that competition among the élites had reached crisis point
by the middle of the sixteenth century. One of these is that the numbers
of the élites were increasing more rapidly than the rest of the
population, particularly after 1500, because the economic conditions
favoured them. For this reason women in the élite groups were able to
marry earlier at the age of 20–21, while women in the lower orders were
marrying later at the age of 27–8. This meant that élite families were
having 4.5 children on average, while the non-élites were only averag-
ing two children. There certainly is evidence to show that the size of
élite families was increasing by the middle of the century. For example,
William Hyde esquire of Denchworth in Berkshire, who died in 1557,
had thirteen surviving children, and his eldest son had ten children.
Even so, doubts are expressed about what effect such developments
would have had by 1558. In 1500 it has been estimated that there were
55 nobles, 500 knights, 800 esquires and 5,000 gentlemen. By 1550
there were still 55 nobles and 500 knights. Although the numbers of
esquires and gentlemen had risen, it is thought unlikely that the rate of
increase greatly exceeded the general population growth of one per cent
per year. It is now considered that, given the buoyant economic
conditions of mid-Tudor England, any increases in numbers would
have been insufficient to cause any real problems. However, it is
thought that large élite families may well have been one of the causes of
the social tensions building up by 1600.

The most widely held view has been that the rising gentry, whether
or not they can be considered to have been what Marxist historians term
the bourgeoisie, were in conflict with the aristocracy. This theory runs

alongside that of the revisionist historians, who see the gentry in political conflict with the aristocracy for places in central and local government. It has been estimated that in 1500 the nobility had an average income of £1,000 a year in comparison with £130 for knights, £58 for esquires and £14 for gentlemen. There are no similar estimates for the middle of the century, but it is thought that the incomes for all four groups increased at approximately the same rate. However, there were wide disparities of wealth within each rank. For example, by 1548 Somerset had an income of £7,400 a year from his estates, and a further £5,000 annually from public funds for his office as Lord Protector. Much of his personal wealth came from his success in acquiring ecclesiastical property. Fellow members of the Privy Council – Dudley, Herbert, Paget, Russell, Rich and Wriothesley – had similarly enriched themselves with church lands. Other aristocratic incomes varied from some £3,000 to £4,000 a year down to a few hundred pounds a year. Former gentry families like the Seymours and Dudleys, through a combination of military careers, royal favour, public office and the seizure of church lands, had risen rapidly to the top ranks of the social hierarchy. Such success was exceptional, and must be seen merely as part of the traditional pattern of rising and falling fortune among the élites. Former suggestions that Henry VII and Henry VIII deliberately tried to change the social composition of the aristocracy by promoting new families at the expense of the ancient nobility are now thought to be unfounded. At a county level, fortune among the gentry was just as varied. In north Berkshire three of the established knightly families, the Fettiplaces, Essexes and Norreys, were the most successful in accumulating church land. By 1553 the Fettiplaces had increased their landed income only marginally from £182 a year in 1522 to £184, the Essexes' income had risen from £160 to £238, and the Norreys' land in Berkshire actually fell in value from £142 to £113, but they had been acquiring land in neighbouring Oxfordshire. Another family, the Yates, who were merchants on the fringes of gentility in 1522, increased their landholding from £22 to £122 over the same period. Most of the north Berkshire gentry had not acquired church lands by 1553. For example, the ancient family of Pusey, with one manor worth three pounds in 1522, still had the same amount of land in 1553.

*Success or failure was by no means dependent upon the ability to buy church property. Old noble families such as the Percies, Nevilles and Poles, had fallen through royal disfavour. Others, like the Howards, survived the displeasure of the monarchy to rise again. The Brandon family, which had risen rapidly through royal marriage, fell back into obscurity because it failed to produce male heirs. Families such as the Spencers were establishing themselves through their success in sheep raising and other commercial enterprises. Among the higher clergy, men like Cranmer, Gardiner and Pole continued to exercise considerable political influence, although not on the scale of Thomas

Wolsey earlier in the century. Among the lesser élites it is still not altogether clear whether the office-holding 'court' gentry, or the rural 'mere' gentry were the most successful. The subsequent histories of the five Berkshire families already mentioned are good examples in the variations in fortune. The Fettiplaces had enjoyed considerable royal favour through offices at Court until the middle of the century. However, by then they were heavily in debt, and tried to recoup their losses by purchasing land so that they could take advantage of the expected inflation in land values. At the same time they supported Somerset in his rise to power and, after his execution in 1552, they fell out of Court favour. During the second half of the sixteenth century they were forced to sell more of their estates and never regained their former eminence. The long-established Essex family also speculated in land, with even less success, and they had become bankrupt by 1600. In contrast the Norreys were very successful in their land dealings, and, through royal favour under Elizabeth, they rose to become the Earls of Banbury in Oxfordshire. In spite of being strong Catholic sympathisers the Yates consolidated their position in the ranks of the gentry. The Pusey family demonstrated that in the favourable economic conditions it was possible to prosper even without acquiring additional land. In 1522 Thomas Pusey's wealth had been estimated at eight pounds. When his grandson Philip died in 1573 he left £238 in his will. This represents an increase of over 2,800 per cent in 50 years, whereas the rate of inflation was only 200 per cent over the same period.

*In the buoyant conditions of mid-Tudor England there appears to be little reason to suppose that there was sufficient social rivalry between the gentry and the aristocracy to amount to a crisis. Life was still a wheel of fortune, but there were ample opportunities for advancement for the enterprising individual. In any case it is difficult to see why there should be serious antagonism between the gentry and the aristocracy at this juncture. Most of the gentry were members of well-established families descended from, and related by marriage to, the aristocracy. It was during the second half of the century, when many more commercial and professional families began to acquire country estates, that the composition of the gentry began to become more bourgeois. In 1558 the élites still appear to have been a closely-knit group, bound together by their belief in their social superiority and their right to rule by birth.

*Marxist historians consider that the emergence of a bourgeoisie was the cause of class conflict leading to social crisis. It is suggested that the Protestant work ethic became the philosophy of this new class. As such it came into conflict with the élite ideals of leisure, ostentatious display, lavish hospitality and high spending. However, by 1558 it seems unlikely that the Protestant work ethic would have had time to establish itself in England, let alone cause conflict. Even if the Protestant work ethic had started to develop, it is difficult to identify a group that would have adopted it, and have been in conflict with the élites. Another reason suggested for such a conflict is the social resentment caused by the nobility's attitudes of superiority. Certainly Sir Thomas Smith's view that the 'fourth sort or class' were of no account and only there to be ruled does seem provocative. The élites were insistent that due deference had to be paid to them. The sumptuary laws (a code which set out the clothes to be worn by, and the proper conduct of, each rank in society, first introduced in 1363) were regularly re-enacted during the sixteenth century. However, by the middle of the century there were only three groups that might have been influenced by such consideration: the clergy, the urban élites and the yeomen.

Of the three groups that held the middle ground of society in mid-Tudor England, the clergy were the least likely to be bourgeois, or to have caused social conflict. The clerical hierarchy had not changed by 1558, and its status in society rested on professional and spiritual considerations. The loyalties of the higher clergy, by birth and inclination, were still with the élites. For the same reasons the lower clergy felt a greater affinity towards the non-élites. Even so, only a minority joined in popular uprisings such as the Western Rebellion. The majority still believed that society was God-ordained and that rebellion was a mortal sin.

The urban élites seem to be the most likely candidates for an emerging bourgeoisie, and for resentment with élite pretensions to superiority. They formed a more individualistic and competitive group outside the rural social structure. For them hard work and thrift were important. There is little question that many of them did resent the position of social inferiority imposed on them by the élites, but it is very doubtful that this amounted to serious social conflict in mid-Tudor England. The urban hierarchies had remained virtually unaffected by the changes that had taken place within rural society. Each town still had its own inward-looking hierarchy, and there is little sign that a national urban identity, amounting to bourgeois class consciousness, had yet emerged. The main ambition of wealthy merchants and industrialists was still to join the ranks of the élites by purchasing country estates. Urban élites appear to have been just as anxious to avoid any social unrest that might threaten their position as their rural counterparts. In 1549 cities such as Norwich and Exeter supported the government in resisting the popular rebellions.

The exact position of yeomen in society is more difficult to define. Sir Thomas Smith clearly considered them to be part of the minor élites. Historians consider that what distinguished yeomen from the lesser gentry was that they worked their own land and avoided ostentatious display. However, some yeomen were called, and liked to call themselves, gentlemen. Equally many were proud to be known as yeomen. For example Thomas Blagrove, who died in 1583, left £381 in his will, which made him wealthier than many of his gentry neighbours, but he still termed himself a yeoman. The yeomen were not a new group in society, but were merely more numerous by the mid-sixteenth century. Traditionally they had formed the backbone of rural society, and acted as intermediaries between the mass of the population and the ruling élites. This explains why Robert Kett, a wealthy Norfolk yeoman, was hanged for rebellion in 1549. He considered that he was acting as a spokesman for the rebels, and supporting the government by drawing attention to the abuse of political power by the Norfolk gentry who were failing to carry out Privy Council instructions over enclosures (see page 111). In general historians consider that there is no evidence of conflict between the rising yeomen and the élites.

*There seems to be no real evidence to suggest that a bourgeoisie had emerged in England by the middle of the sixteenth century. Nor does there seem to have been any social conflict between the middle and upper ranks of society. The landowning élites, the clergy, yeomen and urban élites all appear to have been united in maintaining the ideal of social stability.

*If there was social conflict and crisis in mid-Tudor England, the popular uprisings of 1549 appear to suggest that it was caused by problems among the lower orders. The difficulty is to decide whether the problems were caused by social tensions. Lower order society had been evolving for 200 years since the beginning of the feudal crisis. Its structure had been created by the people themselves taking advantage of the improved economic conditions of the fifteenth century, and had not been imposed on them by the élites. Historians see no reason why the comparatively stable, non-élite society of the 1520s should have radically altered by the middle of the century. The problem is seen to lie in the economic conditions, which no longer favoured the lower orders. Rising population and inflation brought prosperity to the élites, and eroded the standard of living for the non-élites – a situation on which one of the early pioneering social historians commented: 'Villeinage [serfdom] ceases but the poor laws begin'.

There is ample evidence to support such an interpretation of the problems in 1549. It is estimated that the population was rising at the rate of one per cent per year, and possibly faster, up to the middle of the century. This would have meant that the fairly comfortable population level of 2.3 million in 1522 may well have reached some three million by 1550. This, it is thought, might well have put a strain on food production and produced a Malthusian crisis, which was made worse by the harvest failure in 1549. The greater number of people enabled landowners to push up the level of rents, and employers to keep down wages. In contrast, inflation, which is estimated to have run at four per cent per year over the whole country, was compounded by the debasements of the coinage in the 1540s (see page 30) and may well have reached over 200 per cent by 1550. For the growing number of wage-earners the situation was made worse by the collapse of the

Antwerp cloth market (see page 136), resulting in heavy job losses in the country's largest industry. Furthermore, the comparative lack of popular unrest in the 1550s can be explained by heavy mortality caused by severe epidemics of plague and 'sweating sickness' in 1551 and 1552, and influenza in 1558, which relieved population pressure.

In the past a number of historians have considered the popular rebellions of 1549 to be clear proof of social conflict directed particularly against the gentry. It is true that in the West Country and in Norfolk the rebels were antagonistic towards the local gentry. The Privy Council described both uprisings as social conflict which threatened to undermine the whole fabric of society. However, historians now regard such statements as government propaganda intended to unite the élites behind an increasingly unpopular administration. Much of the resentment towards the gentry centred on the accusation that they were using the Reformation to enrich themselves and to exploit their tenants. But, as it has been suggested, historians see little reason why the sale of church lands should have had any great effect upon the tenants. Another major cause of resentment was that the rebels, like the government, mistakenly blamed enclosure for the adverse economic situation. It is difficult to see how this could have had an immediate effect in 1549. The great bulk of enclosures had taken place before 1520, and most of it was in the Midlands, where there were no popular uprisings. Clearly enclosure did have a social effect in altering the pattern of community life in the villages, but it was part of the changes that had been in progress since the end of the fourteenth century. In any case, much of the enclosure had been carried out by mutual consent among the husbandmen, to improve agricultural production.

*It is now suggested that such apparently social conflict was really the reaction of the masses to economic hardship. During the sixteenth century it is estimated that at least 50 per cent of the rural and urban non-élites lived on, or below, the poverty line – even in good years. Discontent, therefore, was always just below the surface, and broke into revolt at times of widespread unemployment and food shortages, such as in 1549. On such occasions the ruling élites were accused of economic and political exploitation. Of course it can be said that this was a social crisis, because the élites were responsible for maintaining a social structure which placed them in a highly privileged position. However, it must be remembered that the social structure of the rural lower orders in the mid-sixteenth century had been created when they had had the economic advantage in the fifteenth century. It is suggested that the rural rebels were largely illiterate and inarticulate, and relied on rumour and hearsay to explain problems which they did not understand. For this reason local issues and grievances became of paramount importance, and the past became a vanished 'golden age' of prosperity to which they wished to return. Consequently, many of the grievances of such uprisings belonged more to a 'folk memory' of past events rather than to current issues. Kett's rebellion in Norfolk is a good example of this interpretation. East Anglia was the most densely populated and highly industrialised part of the country. Norwich was the second largest town after London, and was a major textile centre. The causes of the rebellion are symptomatic of the nature of lower order discontent against social and economic change. The rising was triggered by unrest over enclosures. East Anglia had a large number of independent small farmers, who were being adversely affected by gentry and yeomen enclosing fields and commons. At the same time the collapse of textile exports had thrown large numbers of clothworkers in Norwich and the surrounding countryside out of work. In June there were riots at the neighbouring market towns of Attleborough and Wymondham, and some new fences put up by Sir John Flowerdew were pulled down. Flowerdew was a lawyer who had bought up church property in the area. This made him unpopular with the locals, who resented him as an outsider. Furthermore he was in dispute with the townspeople of Wymondham over the local abbey, which he had bought and was pulling down. The townspeople had bought the abbey church for use by the parish, and were incensed when Flowerdew began to strip the lead from the roof. Flowerdew was also in dispute with Robert Kett, a local yeoman, over land. Kett himself had enclosed much of the common at Wymondham, and Flowerdew tried to turn the rioters against him. Kett, in the tradition of good neighbourliness, turned the tables by offering to act as spokesman for the rioters. He quickly gathered an army of 16,000 men, and in July was able to capture Norwich. Like the other popular uprisings (see page 75), the rebellion was eventually crushed, and Kett was hanged for sedition.

1 *Articles of the Norfolk Rebels 1549*
We pray your grace that where it is enacted for enclosing [legislation against enclosure] that it be not hurtful to such as enclosed . . . and that henceforth no man shall enclose any more.
5 We pray that Redeground [grassland] and meadow grounds may be at such price as they were in the first year of King Henry the VII.
We pray that all freeholders and copyholders may take the profits of all commons, and there to common, and the lords not to
10 common nor take profits from the same.
We pray that copyhold land that is not reasonably rented may go as it did in the first year of King Henry VII and that at the death of a tenant or of a sale of the same lands to be charged with an easy fine as a capon [a light down payment such as a chicken] or a
15 reasonable sum of money for a remembrance [token].
We pray that all bond men [serfs] may be free for God made all free with his precious blood shedding.

We pray that rivers may be free and open to all men for fishing and passage.

There were sixteen more articles, covering a range of topics, such as sea fishing, dovecots, rabbits, bullocks, and priests, who were also seen by the rebels as exploiting the economic situation. The six articles given above are quite typical of the remainder. The first is interesting because, apart from local incidents such as at Wymondham and Attleborough, there had been relatively few enclosures in Norfolk during the previous 50 years. Similarly, the request that serfs should be made free seems to be going back to past struggles, because there is no evidence that there were any unfree peasants in sixteenth-century Norfolk. The major demands were for commons to be kept open and free for the husbandmen to graze their livestock, and that rents should not be increased excessively. Just as the West Country rebels seemed to wish for religion to be returned to the good old days of Henry VIII, the Norfolk insurgents appeared to yearn for the favourable economic conditions that existed under Henry VII. This does seem to support the notion that the major cause of the popular unrest in 1549 was the harsh economic conditions that prevailed in that year.

Mid-sixteenth century English society appears to have been in an early stage of the evolution from feudal to capitalist. There was considerable underlying continuity, although significant differences had emerged. Society appears to have reached a point where the changes taking place over the previous two centuries had been consolidated. English society was about to enter the next phase of its development, which was to bring even greater structural change. At this point any stresses appear to have come from potential crises in the economy, rather than a crisis in society.

The Feudal Social Hierarchy c. 1350

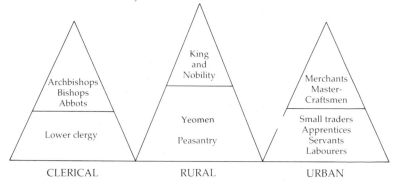

| CLERICAL | RURAL | URBAN |

(a) Summary – A Crisis in Society?

The Early Tudor Social Hierarchy *c.* 1550

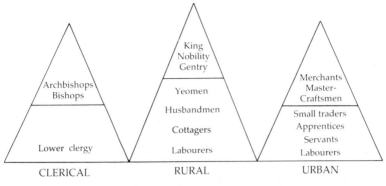

CLERICAL   RURAL   URBAN

(b) Summary – A Crisis in Society?

Making notes on 'A Crisis in Society?'

The purpose of this chapter is to trace the emergence of early capitalistic society, and to see whether this process had created a crisis in mid-Tudor England. Your notes should give you a clear picture of the sequence of structural changes within society between the fourteenth century and the middle of the sixteenth century. You must think carefully about the significance of the changes at each stage of this evolution. Similarly your notes should set out the case for and against a mid-Tudor social crisis, and you must make your own judgement as to the validity of the arguments on both sides. The following headings and questions should help you organise your thinking about the topic:

1. Introduction.
1.1. What are the difficulties in measuring social change?
1.2. What are the major Marxist theories of social change?
1.3. What is the revisionist theory of social change?
1.4. How is the Reformation seen as influencing social change?
1.5. Why do many historians disagree with these general theories, and how do they account for social change?
1.6. Is there any evidence for a mid-Tudor social crisis?
2. Social Mobility and the Social Structure.
2.1. What are the difficulties in measuring social change, and how do historians try to overcome them?
2.2. What social models do historians construct for late medieval English society?

2.3. What forms of social mobility existed among the landed élites, the peasantry and in the towns? How did the Church and the towns help social mobility?

3. Early Tudor Society.

3.1. What effect did the feudal crisis have upon the social hierarchies? How were the social structure and forms of mobility of the rural élite changed? How were the social structure and forms of mobility of the rural lower orders changed?

3.2. What was the social impact of the Renaissance?

3.3. What was the shape of rural society by the 1520s? What difficulties are there in measuring social change between the 1520s and the 1550s?

3.4. What was the social impact of the Reformation? What effect did the re-distribution of church lands have upon the social structure by 1558?

3.5. How accurate a social model have historians constructed for mid-Tudor England?

4. A Social Crisis 1547–58?

4.1. What evidence is there for social competition among the élites? What evidence is there for conflict between the gentry and the aristocracy?

4.2. What were the causes of success or failure among the élites?

4.3. Is there any evidence for the emergence of a bourgeoisie, and, if so, from which section of society was it formed?

4.4. Why is it more likely that it was economic rather than social problems that were responsible for popular unrest?

4.5. What were the causes and outcome of the Kett Rebellion? How far do the demands of the Norfolk rebels suggest that popular discontent in 1549 was economic rather than social?

Source-based questions on 'A Crisis in Society?'

1 Shellingford in 1522
Study the extract from the muster certificate for Shellingford, which includes all the details about individuals (page 101). Answer the following questions:

a) Why was the muster certificate drawn up? (2 marks)

b) How accurate was it likely to be? (2 marks)

c) Assuming that the average family numbered 4.5, how many people lived in the village? (2 marks)

d) Assuming that movable property to the value of four pounds and above indicates a self-sufficient family, how many people in the village would have depended on wages for part of their income? Explain your answer. (4 marks)

2 The structure of society in 1565

Read the extract from Sir Thomas Smith's *The Commonwealth of England* given on pages 104–5. Answer the following questions:

a) Explain the meaning of 'the port, charge and countenance of a gentleman' (line 13). (3 marks)
b) What are the four classes of society that Smith identifies? (4 marks)
c) To which class does Smith probably belong? Explain your answer. (4 marks)
d) How reliable is this extract as evidence of the structure of mid-Tudor society? (3 marks)
e) Of what is the extract reliable evidence? (2 marks)

3 The Norfolk Rebels of 1549

Read the extract from the articles of the Norfolk rebels, given on pages 111–12, and answer the following questions:

a) What is meant by (i) 'commons' (line 9) and (ii) 'copyhold land' (line 11)? (2 marks)
b) What evidence does the extract provide to support the view that 'the rebels were primarily reacting against a worsening economic situation'? (6 marks)
c) What is surprising about the fifth article (lines 16–17)? What can be deduced from its inclusion? (4 marks)
d) Why were the rebels unsuccessful in obtaining redress for their grievances? (4 marks)

CHAPTER 6

A Crisis in the Economy?

1 Introduction

Economic historians, like their social counterparts, are no longer content merely to describe the economy as it existed in the past. Instead they investigate and analyse the structural changes taking place, and try to identify the mechanisms creating the changes. Because economic and social development are so closely linked, some economic historians use the same broad theories to explain the transition from feudalism to capitalism. However, others are more interested in identifying the mechanisms which create growth or decline than in considering the social consequences of such variations. For this reason, many economic historians concentrate their attention on calculating how the movement of people altered the balance within the economy. They identify a number of economic sectors, and by measuring the shifts in the number of people employed in different occupations they calculate whether an economy was backward, or advanced. Economies in which most people were employed in agriculture, forestry or fishing are considered to have been the most primitive. Once a distinct movement of human resources out of these areas into a more economically advanced sector (such as manufacturing) can be discerned, then the economy is considered to have been expanding. So, if by the middle of the sixteenth century there was a movement of people out of agriculture into industry, the English economy could be considered to be growing. In theory this sounds easy, but, of course, in practice it is much less simple.

The difficulty is that there are other considerations to be taken into account. If people were moving out of agriculture then they were becoming less self-sufficient, and more dependent upon the food markets. This meant that agriculture had to be more efficient to produce enough food to support the increasing number of wage-earners. At the same time sixteenth-century industry mainly used raw materials, such as wool, wood and leather, produced by agriculture. Consequently, if industry was to expand, more raw materials had to be produced. However, the danger was that agriculture might prove to be unable to produce either enough food or sufficient raw materials. If this were the case there would be food shortages, a slump in industry, and economic decline. The question of whether or not there was a mid-century economic crisis hinges very much on this issue.

*There is considerable debate and disagreement over the nature of the changes in the English economy in the first half of the sixteenth century. Many economic historians consider that the theories and techniques of economists and social scientists are not helpful in analysing pre-industrial economies. It is felt that they are too preoccupied with trying to explain the Industrial Revolution of the late eighteenth century as an inevitable process dating from the sixteenth century. The emphasis placed by Marxist historians on the emergence of capitalism being the result of changes in economic relationships is considered to be too generalised. Non-Marxist economic historians stress the wide range of local and regional variations, which make general theories virtually meaningless. Equally, the absence of reliable data makes it very difficult to quantify economic growth or decline in the past with any accuracy. Apart from these debates there is considerable controversy between the evolutionary and revolutionary schools of thought. The evolutionists see the economy progressing through a series of small, almost imperceptible changes, within great underlying continuity. In contrast, the revolutionists consider that the economy advanced by well-marked stages, through bursts of technological activity. Between these extremes, economic historians select a variety of explanations of economic advance or decline. For some, developments in agriculture, industry or overseas trade are of paramount importance. Equally, emphasis is placed by other historians on the effects of intervention by the State, variations in population levels, inflation and the influence of towns.

  * It is frequently very difficult to decide which of these approaches is most useful in determining the state of the economy in the middle of the sixteenth century. It is argued that as the country was still overwhelmingly rural, changes in agriculture must be seen as of prime importance. A strong case has been made for there having been an agricultural revolution in the sixteenth century, based upon commercialisation and new techniques. Evolutionists reject this idea on the basis that the use of fresh skills was on too small a scale and too localised to be revolutionary, although they do agree that there was greater capitalistic input. This, in turn, can be interpreted as either resulting from the emergence of the gentry and the yeomen, or being brought about by the entrepreneurial influence of merchants buying country estates. While there are strong arguments in favour of the importance of urban influence in creating economic growth in the countryside, other historians regard this as a time of 'urban crisis' and recession. Many historians consider that the agricultural expansion of the early sixteenth century was the natural result of population growth and inflation. However, it must be remembered that in a pre-industrial economy a sharp demographic increase could equally lead to overpopulation, poverty, and a subsistence crisis.

  The situation in the industrial sector is just as vexed. Here, too, it has been suggested that there was a revolution, based in this instance on the coal industry, which caused a decisive shift towards capitalistically intensive, heavy production. Although there is little support among modern historians for the idea of a sixteenth-century industrial revolution, it is agreed that industry was becoming more capitalistic. What is in dispute is the form of commercial development that was taking place. Many argue that the so-called 'proto-industrial' growth in cottage industry was highly significant. While the general growth theory of proto-industrialisation leading eventually to the late eighteenth-century factory system is widely contested, the importance of the rural cottage industry is still generally accepted. However, other historians still maintain that the development of capitalistically intensive fixed plant, such as mills and furnaces, was more significant. Even the question of measuring the movement of the workforce into more economically advanced sectors is regarded as very difficult. Any shifts depend upon such variables as the mobility of labour, the availability of capital and technology and the existence of effective transport and communications. Moreover, such conditions are seen as being dependent on government attitudes. The State, as the largest investor in the economy, is regarded as a major promoter of economic growth. However, State intervention, with legislation against enclosures and vagrancy, can be seen as inhibiting commercialisation.

*Another method of assessing possible structural change is to examine the English economy in the wider context of western Europe and the development of world trade. England is seen as forming part of the western European, pre-industrial economy, but is regarded as a backward offshore island in the first half of the sixteenth century. The whole of this economy is seen as being labour intensive, with low levels of production and little fixed capital. Demand is considered to have been inelastic in that it could only be increased by creating new markets outside Europe, rather than by expanding trade within the existing home market. Compared with the continent, the English economy is considered to have been deficient in almost every respect. In commercial terms, England, apart from the sale of semi-finished cloth, was an exporter of raw materials and an importer of manufactured and luxury goods. Moreover, it was not until after the 1560s that England is seen as playing any significant part in the development of the world trade routes pioneered by Spain and Portugal. In terms of agriculture, industry and commerce, the Netherlands is regarded as being much more advanced than England. German mining techniques and heavy industry, and the textile industries in France, Italy and Spain are considered far superior in quality and technology to their English counterparts. However, the first half of the sixteenth century is thought by many economic historians to be a time when England began to catch up with the continent. For this reason the middle of the century can be seen as an important watershed – a turning point – in economic terms. The difficulties and restructuring of the first part of the century are considered to have produced conditions suitable for a renewal of modest economic growth. However, what needs to be estimated is whether the mid-century English economy experienced a crisis in reaching this position and, if so, what was the nature and extent of the problem.

*Much of the controversy over the state of the economy is caused by the nature of the evidence. There was no systematic record-keeping in sixteenth-century England, and this makes it difficult to quantify the available data. The evidence that does exist is fragmentary, unreliable, and often unsuitable for quantification. A good example of the problem is the taxation and muster listings, such as the muster certificates for 1522 (see page 101), which historians use to calculate population levels. A major shortcoming of such lists is that, although originally drawn up on a national basis, many of the returns have been lost, so that it is impossible to obtain a full picture for the whole country. In any case these listings were made to record the number of men available for military service, or to assess taxation. For this reason they generally only record men and heads of households who were liable to pay tax. This means that it is necessary to calculate the number of women and children and other dependants who made up the normal household. Many historians accept that a reasonable estimate of population can be obtained by multiplying the listed heads of household by 4.5. However, not all historians agree that this is the best multiplier, and there is considerable debate as to what percentage (between ten and thirty per cent) should be added to represent the poor who were not included in the listings. Similar problems apply to parish registers. In addition, the cause of death was rarely recorded in burial registers. This, along with the lack of medical knowledge in Tudor England, makes it very difficult to calculate mortality rates and the extent and nature of epidemics. Records from all the other areas of the economy are equally problematical. Weights and measures, wage rates, the size of textiles and methods of calculating imports and exports varied widely across the country so that it is almost impossible to get a clear picture of the economy. For these reasons the existing interpretations must be regarded as very provisional.

2 Population, Inflation and the Standard of Living

There is considerable debate over the changing rates of population growth during the sixteenth century, particularly in the period between 1500 and 1550. At the beginning of the fourteenth century it is estimated that the population of England was as high as six million. After the Black Death of 1349 and the subsequent plague cycle it is thought that the population might have fallen to as low as 1.5 million by 1460. Demographers see this decline as the major cause of the deflation and recession of the fifteenth century. From about 1470 it is thought that the population had begun to recover, reaching some 2.3 million by the 1520s. There is broad agreement about this pattern of demographic decline and recovery, but not about the causes for the revival. There is little dispute that the bubonic plague, carried by the fleas of the black rat, was the cause of the initial catastrophic population losses. What is less clear is what caused the recovery after 1470. Bubonic plague was still endemic, along with a number of other diseases such as influenza, cholera, malaria and typhus. This makes it difficult to maintain that a fall in the rate of mortality was a major reason for a re-growth in population. However, some historians consider that people were beginning to build up immunity to some forms of disease. Others suggest that vulnerability to epidemics varied and changed between age groups. It is claimed that the reason for recovery in population levels could have been that young adults were becoming less susceptible to diseases. If more young women survived, increased numbers of children were likely to be born, which would account for a rise in population. Alternatively it is claimed that there was a drop in infant mortality, which similarly would have led to a rise in the demographic levels.

*The situation between the 1520s and 1558 is equally uncertain. It is estimated that the population was growing at approximately one per cent per year until 1550, when it possibly just exceeded three million. However, the rate of expansion was not even. It is suggested that there was only a very slow improvement until 1540, followed by rapid growth over the next decade, and that by 1558 population levels were falling back again. Once again there is no single explanation for this pattern of events. It is suggested that a major factor was the presence of endemic disease. From the end of the fifteenth century a new virus had joined the killer diseases that were already present. The 'English sweat', a fever which spread more quickly than the plague, was particularly virulent between 1485 and 1528, and could kill within 24 hours. It struck particularly at young adults, and it is thought that this, by reducing the birthrate, slowed the rate of population increase up to 1540. Moreover there were four serious outbreaks of plague between 1500 and 1528, and another in the late 1530s, to which adolescents were especially vulnerable. However, it is felt that the comparative absence of epidemics between 1528 and 1550 might well account for the sharp demographic increase in the 1540s. Again, it is suggested that a fall in infant mortality might have been a major cause for more children surviving into adulthood. It is even felt by some historians that the Reformation might have led to a rise in population: Protestant clergy were allowed to marry and so produce children. However, the effect of this is thought to have been marginal, and unlikely to have had any impact by the 1540s.

The substantial check to population increase in the 1550s is easier to explain. In 1551 and 1552 there were fresh outbreaks of plague and sweating sickness. Even more serious was the influenza epidemic which ravaged the whole country between 1556 and 1558. It is estimated that it had a mortality rate of at least six per cent, and that the population might have been reduced to under three million. All these figures are very speculative and are based on the uncertain evidence of taxation returns and parish registers. To add to the difficulties of obtaining a clear picture, there were considerable local variations in population densities, the rate of increase or decline, and in the incidence of disease. In broad terms the south-eastern section of England was more heavily populated than the north-west because of the different farming regions (see page 126). Towns, particularly London, which had high concentrations of people, were especially susceptible to epidemics, but the rate of recovery was normally rapid. East Anglia was the most highly populated area, while the north of England had the least number of people per square mile. In sparsely settled areas epidemics were less likely, but the rate of recovery from any population losses was slower.

★ There is ample evidence from empty houses and abandoned plots of land in both towns and villages that the population during the first half of the sixteenth century had not recovered from earlier losses. In north Berkshire the village of Hinton, even by 1573, had not recovered the level of population that it had in 1381. In contrast, a survey of the nearby market town of Wantage in the 1550s estimated that the town's population was 1,000; a figure confirmed by calculations from the parish registers. This compares with a population of 600 in 1522 – a rise of 66 per cent over 30 years, and twice the estimated national average. The level of increase in the neighbouring villages was lower, and in some cases there was an actual decrease. It is very difficult to pinpoint the causes of such discrepancies in the countryside, and between villages within a few miles of each other. Much of the similarly varied demographic fortunes of towns in early Tudor England can be attributed to the random outbreak of disease. The three largest towns after London – Norwich, Bristol and York – all suffered severe epidemics in the middle of the century. Indeed, it is calculated that the population of Norwich remained stationary between 1522 and 1558, which is in marked contrast to the growth of London and some other towns.

★ The evidence of population levels in the mid-sixteenth century is complicated, and often contradictory. Nevertheless, a number of historians consider that there may have been overpopulation by 1549, leading to a subsistence, or Malthusian crisis. Although the level of population, even at its height in about 1550, was only about half that which had been supported early in the fourteenth century, a number of reasons are advanced to justify this interpretation. The weather is considered to have deteriorated since the end of the thirteenth century. Temperature levels are estimated to have fallen by two degrees centigrade, and the annual rainfall to have increased. Consequently the growing season is considered to have shortened. These conditions are thought to have persisted throughout the sixteenth century, with alternating spells of good and bad weather. The result was that there were sequences of good, and very poor harvests. There were bad harvests from 1527 to 1529, 1549 to 1551 and 1554 to 1556, although historians consider that only the exceptionally bad harvests of 1555 and 1556 were poor enough to produce an actual dearth, or famine, on a wide scale. However, there were problems at a local level, such as the chronic food shortages in Coventry during the 1520s and possibly at Norwich in 1532. There were good harvests from 1537 to 1542, and 1546 to 1548. The poor harvests in the 1520s and 1550s coincided with epidemics and probably worsened the mortality rate, while the plague epidemic of the late 1530s occurred during a run of good harvests. These are seen as accentuating the underlying demographic trend. The almost unbroken run of good harvests up to 1548 would have lowered grain prices, and so have raised living standards for the mass of the population. In turn, this may have encouraged earlier marriage, and so intensified the upward spiral in population by 1549.

Paradoxically, low grain prices, enclosures and the increasing commercialisation of farming (which are seen as economically progressive) may well have made the situation worse (see page 125). Enclosed and other land, which could have been used to raise cereals, was being used to produce wool and other high value crops. Such practices, combined with greater regional specialisation, may well have created local shortages, made worse by the inadequate transport system. Population pressure in 1549–50 and underlying food shortages are seen as possible contributing factors to the level of popular discontent. By the mid-1550s when the run of harvests was even worse, population pressure had been eased by the epidemics in 1551 and 1552, and other causes for unrest were less evident. Much of the hostility towards the gentry in Norfolk in 1549 is thought to have arisen because of the conversion of arable land into sheep pasture. This may have created local grain shortages. However, it is possible that anger was aroused among husbandmen because they felt that gentry competition was undermining their own agricultural specialisation (see page 129). Whether or not there was a subsistence problem by 1549, the sharp increase in the population during the 1540s helps to explain the government's anxieties over enclosures and vagrancy. It was part of a desire by the authorities, which continued into the 1550s, to see more husbandmen on the land and an increase in the acreage of arable under cultivation.

*Inflation, which is estimated to have been 400 per cent over the whole of the century, is seen as another major contributor to the economic pressures that existed by the middle of the century. In the past it was thought that the large amount of silver imported by Spain into western Europe from South America was the major cause of inflation in the sixteenth century. This view is no longer widely held, and it is thought that South American silver had little effect on English inflation until the end of the century. It is widely agreed that rising population, which increased demand, was the underlying cause of inflation. However, this alone does not explain the pattern of inflation during the first half of the century. The 'price scissors', the point when prices and rents overtook wages, is seen as occurring soon after 1500. Prices and rents continued to rise until after 1550, but until 1540 the actual rise in population was slow. Even by the 1530s grain and meat prices were increasing quite rapidly in town markets, and may have doubled between 1510 and 1530. Historians attribute this trend in part to the poor harvests of the 1520s, but prices showed no sign of falling even by the late 1520s after a run of good harvests. The reason for this, it is thought, was that commercial farmers were still concentrating on pasture for wool production. This, and enclosure, are seen to be the underlying causes for the upward spiral of rents. By the 1540s population pressure added to the upward movement of inflation.

Other forces were at work to create high inflation by 1550. Debasements of the coinage, which began in 1526, became very frequent in the 1540s, when the government was desperately trying to raise money to finance the wars against France and Scotland (see page 30). By increasing the amount of money in circulation while devaluing the coinage, debasement caused very rapid inflation of prices. At the same time the Reformation may well have contributed to this process. Gold and silver ornaments, seized from the monasteries, chantries and churches, were melted down and turned into coins, so adding to the volume of debased coinage in circulation. By 1550 the rate of inflation may have reached 200 per cent over the first half of the century, and the very high levels of inflation reached by 1549 may well have contributed to the widespread popular discontent. By 1553 epidemics had eased population pressure and so slowed the rate of inflation. At the same time, government reforms of the currency reduced the amount of debased coinage in circulation. The effect was to reduce the rate of inflation still further, which might help to explain the lack of popular unrest during the bad harvests of the mid-1550s.

*The levels of rents and wages are seen as another possible contributor to popular unrest, because they too had a direct effect on the standard of living. With relatively sluggish population growth up to 1540, it might be expected that rents and wages would remain comparatively stable. As far as wages were concerned this is exactly what happened. In the south of England the wages for rural workers remained at 4d. a day, and for building workers at 6d. a day, until the 1550s. This meant that the level of wages obtained in the fifteenth century when population was very low, was maintained in spite of the increase in demographic levels. However, because of the considerable increase in inflation, the standard of living of all wage-earners is considered to have fallen. The evidence of the level of rents is less conclusive. In some areas, especially around London, rents were certainly going up by the 1530s, and may even have more than doubled from 6d. per acre to 13d. per acre. In other areas, away from south-eastern England, they appear to have remained static, and in some places may even have fallen slightly. The pressure was heaviest on pasture land because of the demand for wool and other animal products. Enclosed land commanded higher rents, and may have affected levels of rent in the surrounding district.

Although the evidence is not conclusive it is felt that resentment over the level of rents and wages may have added to popular discontent, especially in the southern half of the country. The problem is that there is no clear division between smallholders and labourers. Although it is estimated that over 40 per cent of the population were wage-earners – 10 per cent working in industry – only a minority were full-time employees. Many smallholders supplemented their incomes by wages, and most workers in cottage and other industries had their own smallholdings, or gardens. A large number of town labourers spent part of the year working in the countryside, especially at harvest time. This makes it very difficult to select any one particular cause for economic discontent among the lower orders, and large-scale uprisings may have been caused by groups with different grievances coming together for mutual support.

*In spite of the conflicting evidence there are some clear links between living standards and popular discontent in the middle of the century. Even if the standard of living of the mass of the population had not fallen as dramatically as it was once assumed, it certainly had not improved. Clearly the rebels in Norfolk felt that their economic position had declined since the end of the fifteenth century, and blamed it largely on rising rents (see page 112). The groups who had gained generally from increased rents and prices were the élites, the yeomen, merchants, industrialists, and some husbandmen. Consequently part of the problem in 1549 might have been the general economic resentment of those who felt they were the losers, against those groups which they felt were gaining. However, it must be remembered that it is too simple to make such a clear-cut division. Not everyone in either grouping was either a winner or a loser. Unrest in 1549 was very localised, and a riot or rebellion might have been sparked off by one individual, who thought that his neighbour had cheated him, or was becoming unduly prosperous.

Another way of looking at 1549 is to see it as a particularly bad year, which experienced the conjunction of a number of unrelated problems rather than any one specific difficulty. The bad harvest after a run of good seasons, which pushed up grain prices, would obviously have caused discontent. However, this was not the sole cause, because there was already unrest in 1548 when the harvest was good. A combination of a weak government, mismanaged policies, religious change and reverses in the war had produced an atmosphere of disquiet by 1549. The additional economic problems of high inflation and population pressure may well have turned disquiet into discontent, and open rebellion.

3 Agriculture

As the main occupation in mid-sixteenth-century England, and the employer of the bulk of the population, agriculture had a considerable influence on economic development. Agrarian historians do not see the debate among Marxist historians on the changing nature of relationships within English agriculture as particularly helpful. Instead they see the question of whether agrarian change was revolutionary, or evolutionary, as much more significant. Another major issue of debate is the emergence of regional specialisation and production. Although these topics all have a bearing on the state of mid-century agriculture, it is difficult to say anything precise about agricultural developments over two decades. Even the advocates of revolutionary advances talk in terms of change over a century, or more.

*By the early sixteenth century English agriculture, like society, had been evolving for 200 years since the feudal crisis. In 1300, when the population of England had reached its medieval peak of about six million, it is considered that there was a subsistence crisis, caused by over-population. To support the needs of a growing population farmers must either cultivate more land, or increase the yield per acre of the existing land through new technology and the greater efficiency of the workforce. The limited technology of medieval England meant that as the population had expanded, people were forced to settle and farm areas of grassland and poorer, marginal soil, which was not really suitable for arable cultivation. This, it is thought, upset the balance between arable and pasture, because not enough cattle and sheep were being kept to provide manure for the cultivated land. Lack of manure and the over-cropping of marginal land led to soil exhaustion by the end of the thirteenth century. The situation was made worse by the deterioration in the climate, which rendered uplands even less suitable for arable farming, and river valleys too wet for cultivation. The result was an increasing number of harvest failures culminating in a Malthusian crisis in the early fourteenth century. The Black Death and the subsequent plague cycle ended the situation of over-population, and introduced a new phase of agricultural development.

During the fifteenth century agriculture had no difficulty in feeding the drastically reduced population. This enabled a withdrawal from the more marginal land. Whole areas, such as the Brecklands in Norfolk and Dartmoor in the West Country, were virtually abandoned. In every county many villages on the poorer or wetter soils were deserted, and were never reoccupied. This meant that large tracts of previously cultivated land reverted to grassland and pasture, which enabled more cattle and sheep to be kept. The remaining areas of arable were on the richer soils, or, at least, those soils which would support cultivation with the extra quantity of manure available. Without the constant pressure to produce cereals, farming began to become more specialised. This raises the question as to why England in 1550, with a population of only just over three million, appears to have been barely able to feed this comparatively small number of people. The answer lies in the nature of the changes in agriculture taking place between 1350 and 1550.

*Agrarian historians consider that the increasing diversity of agricultural regions had an important influence over levels of production. There has been considerable debate since the eighteenth century as to what constituted and created a farming region. One of the problems with medieval farming was that it had been dominated by the peasantry. A peasant smallholder had to produce a range of foodstuffs from the land in order to support all the needs of his family. This form of production took no account of the wide variety of soil types or their suitability for general farming. Therefore, peasant cultivation was often inefficient and wasteful. However, even during the Middle Ages, peasants had had to adapt their farming techniques to meet the conditions imposed by moorlands, fens, or forest. After 1350 the reduction in the number of peasant smallholdings meant that gentry, yeomen and husbandmen could begin to specialise within the broader agricultural zones.

*This growing agricultural variety makes it difficult to decide how far farming had progressed by the middle of the sixteenth century. The situation is further complicated because some historians consider that there was an agricultural revolution in the sixteenth century. However, there is disagreement as to whether such a revolution was the result of new techniques, new crops, new methods of field rotation, or enclosure. In any case, many agrarian historians do not think that there was a revolution, and that any changes in agriculture were the result of a very slow process of evolution. Those historians in favour of the idea of a sixteenth-century agricultural revolution point out that a number of new crops, such as clover and lucerne, were introduced to improve fodder for animal feed. Industrial crops such as saffron, woad and rapeseed were being grown to produce dyes and oils for textile manufacture. At the same time it is suggested that improvements were being made to the techniques of breeding cattle and sheep.

A vital part of this process is considered to be the spread of enclosure at the end of the fifteenth century and in the early sixteenth century. This, it is thought, enabled the growth of more efficient median-sized farms, which had flexible field systems. In many parts of the country these new layouts began to replace the old three-field system, where an individual farmer's land was scattered in small plots across the open fields. At the same time much of the common land was enclosed and brought under more intensive cultivation. It was these developments that are considered to have enabled the introduction of greater specialisation and new techniques. 'Up and down husbandry' was a system under which land was used alternatingly over a number of years as arable, and then for pasture. This technique is seen to have prevented soil exhaustion, and to have maintained a better balance between arable and grazing land. Further improvements were made to grazing land by the use of floating water meadows. Here riverside pastures were flooded every year with the aid of sluices so that the river silt would enhance the quality of the grass.

There is wide agreement that all these improvements were taking place at some time, and in some places, during the sixteenth century. However, evolutionists argue very strongly that a few people using some new techniques does not make a revolution. They maintain that any changes were extremely localised, and were only adopted very slowly between 1500 and 1750. Be this as it may, the changes were enabling the development of more specialised farming regions. Unfortunately it is impossible to tell whether this had led to any increase in production by 1550. Agrarian historians suggest that three things were most likely to lead to greater farming output. These were the more efficient commercial farms being created by the gentry and yeomen, the greater acreage of good land brought under cultivation through enclosure, and the introduction of new crops and techniques. However, enclosure and commercialisation were the very things being blamed by the government and its critics for the economic problems in the middle of the sixteenth century.

The possible reason for this apparent paradox is that, although changes were taking place in agriculture, they had not made any appreciable improvement to the levels of cereal production by the mid-century. Indeed, it is considered that in some cases the very changes that were to bring about higher yields later, were the cause of this problem. Enclosures are seen as the major contributor to increased yields. In the first half of the sixteenth century, the gentry and yeomen, who were mainly responsible for enclosure, were clearly looking for the most profitable crops to gain a good return on their investment. During periods of high population grain prices rose, and so enclosed fields, which were ideal for growing cereals, would be used for this purpose. It is thought that in response to rising population, increasing numbers of commercial farmers converted to cereals. By the seventeenth century production was so efficient that grain prices actually fell in spite of a continued rise in population. However, during the first half of the sixteenth century population increase was almost imperceptible until after 1540. For this reason farmers were slow to shift to cereals, preferring to use enclosed land as sheep-runs, so as to profit from high wool prices. Consequently, because of the spurt in population in the 1540s, there may have been localised pressure on grain supplies by 1549.

*Such a view is supported by Sir Thomas Smith in another of his books *A Discourse on the Commonweal of this Realm of England* (see page 104). This takes the form of a dialogue between a doctor, representing the academic view, discussing the state of the economy with various members of society such as a knight, a merchant and a husbandman. After suggesting that the debasing of the coinage had doubled prices in his lifetime, the doctor goes on to discuss the cost and shortage of grain. He suggests that the best way to get more grain was either to make it as expensive as wool, or to reduce the price of wool.

1 *Doctor*: Marry the first way is to make that wool be of as base a price [to] the breeder thereof as corn is; and that shall be, if you make alike restraints of wools, for passing over the sea un-wrought, [unfinished] as ye make corn. [On the other hand]
5 Would you make corn dearer than it is? Have you dearth enough else without that?
Husbandman: I thank you with all my heart; for you have spoken in the matter more [better] than I could do myself . . . We felt the harm, but we wist not what was the cause thereof; many of us
10 saw, 12 years ago, that our profits was small by the plough; and therefore divers [various] of my neighbours that had in times past, some two, some three, some four ploughs of their own, have laid [them] down . . . and turned either part or all their arable ground into pasture, and thereby have waxed very rich men. And
15 every day some of us encloseth a plot of his ground to pasture; and were it not that our ground lieth in the common fields, intermingled one with another, I think also our fields had been enclosed, of a common agreement of all the township [village], long ere this time. And to say the truth, I, that have enclosed little
20 or nothing of my ground, could never be able to make up my lord's rent were it not for a little breed of neat [cattle], sheep, swine, geese, and hens that I do rear upon my ground; whereof, because the price is somewhat round, I make more clear profit than I do of all my corn; and yet I have a bare living, by reason
25 that many things do belong to husbandry which now be exceedingly chargeable over they were in times past.

This view of the economy, speaking as it does of dearth and high corn prices in 1549, supports the idea that there may have been a subsistence crisis in that year. A shortage of grain would not have been entirely due to the under-production of cereals, but, in part, the result of the bad harvest in 1549 following a run of good seasons. What is clear is that it was not just the gentry and yeomen who were failing to grow enough grain, but that husbandmen were equally to blame for any shortfalls. The reason for this appears to have been the low price of grain in comparison with wool and other animal products over the previous decades, which had led to the conversion of arable to pasture. It is interesting to note that husbandmen appear to have been just as keen to enclose their land as the larger commercial farmers, and regarded enclosed holdings as more efficient than the old open fields. Husbandmen clearly were being adversely affected by increased rents and other agricultural overheads. At the same time they were just as ready to react to market forces as the larger commercial farmers. This, along with rising rents, may have been a major cause of popular hostility towards the gentry. Wool was seen as the quickest way of making a profit from land, but sheep-runs were a large-scale undertaking and outside the scope of most husbandmen. It may well have been such commercially-based rivalry that was an important underlying cause of the disorders in 1549.

The willingness of husbandmen to react quickly to market demand and to specialise, particularly in stock-raising, explains why farming regions diversified so quickly. However, the development of a wide range of specialist agricultural regions created a problem in itself. Many such areas were created by the husbandmen responding to local demands and adapting to the types of soil on which they farmed. A good example of this is Wiltshire, where the heavy soils were particularly suited to cattle-raising, and dairy farming became a speciality. Small dairy herds were attractive to husbandmen because they could be managed with family labour, and brought in a regular income from milk, butter and cheese. Larger scale cattle-rearing and fattening was usually outside the scope of the husbandmen because it required more capital investment. Whatever type of specialism was adopted, new agricultural regions created problems for grain supplies during the first part of the sixteenth century. Not only did they lower the overall national level of cereals, but each specialist region became increasingly dependent upon surrounding areas for grain and other farm products. For a regional farming structure to work efficiently a good infrastructure of roads and navigable rivers was needed to move produce quickly from one part of the country to another. The government and local authorities were aware of the problem. Attempts were made to improve river navigation, particularly on the Thames, and local landowners worked with the town authorities to improve roads. However, it is considered that little real progress was made until after the 1560s.

It appears that from the end of the fourteenth century agriculture had diversified and become much less generalised than it had been during the Middle Ages. During the fifteenth century farming became more specialised and efficient in order to cope with the low level of prices. Because of the relatively modest increase in population up to 1540, commercial farmers and husbandmen were slow to respond to the demand for more grain production. This may have caused a temporary, and localised, Malthusian crisis in 1549–50. The reduction in population levels in the 1550s enabled farmers to adjust to higher demands for cereals until at least the end of the century. Clearly food shortages would have added to popular discontent in the middle of the century. Increased rents were another cause of dissatisfaction, but it is apparent that both husbandmen and commercial farmers were practising enclosure. This suggests that the signs of animosity between gentry and husbandmen sprang more from commercial rivalry, than from social divisions.

4 Industry, Commerce and the Urban Crisis

There is just as much debate and controversy among industrial historians as there is among their agrarian colleagues. They, too, have their revolutionary and evolutionary schools of thought. It is generally agreed that during the sixteenth century the essential change was from small-output craft industries controlled by the urban guilds, to large-scale production enterprises directed by entrepreneurial industrialists. However, there is much debate about the nature of the new capitalistic industry. Many historians consider that the spread of the rural putting-out system, mainly using raw materials from agriculture, was most significant. Others feel that heavy industry, based largely on minerals, was the major area of industrial innovation. These issues are further complicated by the debate about whether industries using high cost, capital-intensive machinery, such as mills and furnaces, were more significant than industries such as textiles, which had high labour costs. Other economic historians consider that the development of overseas trade was more important to economic growth than either agriculture or industry. For them the expansion of the Atlantic economy and world trade was the paramount influence on commercial development. A final consideration, thought to be particularly important by historical geographers, is the effect that the varied fortunes of English towns had on the sixteenth-century economy.

All these issues are of great importance in deciding the state of the English economy in the mid-century. However, as they are all so closely interconnected it is very difficult to separate them. As in the case of agriculture, industrial, commercial and urban changes were mainly the consequences of the feudal crisis. This meant that by 1500 there had already been some 200 years of industrial and commercial development that was to set the pattern for the first half of the sixteenth century.

*Some historians regard the changes taking place in the sixteenth century as revolutionary. They see the expansion in the industrial use of non-agricultural raw materials, such as coal and other minerals, as being vitally important in the development of early capitalism. Such operations needed expensive equipment on a centralised site and a small, but highly skilled workforce. Mining and metal-working, along with other specialised and capital-intensive undertakings such as dyeing, brewing, glass and paper-making, are regarded as the real signs of a new, capitalistic economy. Indeed, in the past it has been suggested that the growth of the coal industry in the sixteenth century amounted to an industrial revolution in itself. Most economic historians are now totally sceptical about this concept, and are doubtful about the contribution of heavy industry to the economy before the seventeenth century. Certainly it is true to say that little progress was made in this sector until after 1560.

The basis for 'revolutionary' expansion in the coal industry was the once-popular theory of a timber crisis in sixteenth-century England. This idea is no longer accepted, and it is now thought that any shortages of wood or charcoal were purely local. No sudden rise in the demand for coal can be seen until the end of the sixteenth century. A major problem for expansion in heavy industry was the difficulty and cost of transport. Unlike raw materials from agriculture, coal and other minerals were only to be found in certain areas. Consequently industries associated with these products were very localised because of the cost of carrying heavy materials more than a short distance. It is not considered that any great expansion was possible until improvements to river navigation and sea transport began in the second half of the sixteenth century. Another difficulty preventing the expansion of heavy industry was that English technology was very backward in comparison with that of the continent. Problems of drainage and ventilation meant that mining operations had to be open cast, or through relatively shallow shafts. Coal was mined in south Wales, the Weald of Kent, the Forest of Dean, and parts of the Midlands, but on a small scale for local use. The main coal-producing area was Northumberland and Durham, and increasingly large quantities were shipped to London from the end of the fourteenth century. This 'sea coal' was used largely for domestic fires.

*Before the second half of the sixteenth century only small quantities of coal were used for industrial purposes. The main reason for this, apart from transport costs, was that heavy industry was localised and only used coal if it was mined nearby. Another important consideration was that coal was unsuitable for iron smelting. Iron ore, like coal, was mined in various places, but mainly in the Weald of Kent and the Forest of Dean, where there was a plentiful supply of timber for making charcoal to smelt the ore. At the end of the fifteenth century, gentry and yeomen ironmasters in the Weald began to use a new type of blast furnace, fuelled by charcoal and powered by water, which had been introduced from the continent. By the 1550s, 26 of these new furnaces were in use in the Weald, making it a major producer of cast iron, which was used particularly for making naval guns and shot. However, pig iron was still the major output. This was converted into bar iron in a finery forge, also fuelled by charcoal and driven by water. The bars of iron were then distributed on pack animals to blacksmiths in the towns and villages for making into tools and other small objects. Apart from the technological advance in iron production, little real progress was made elsewhere before 1560. Tin was mined in Devon and Cornwall mainly for export. Much the same can be said for lead and zinc mining in Shropshire and the Mendips. Although a new blast furnace for smelting lead, which only used half as much fuel, was introduced, the metal-working industries were on a very small scale. It was only after the 1570s that copper, pewter, brass and silver production began to become important. Other specialist, centralised industries such as brick, tile and glass-making, bell-founding and gunpowder manufacture, were still very localised. New, sophisticated processes such as paper-making were only just being introduced.

By the mid-sixteenth century heavy industry had had little impact on economic growth, and was still at the stage of catching up with continental technology. However, if this sector cannot be said to have made any positive contribution to industrial expansion, neither can it be considered to have added to the economic problems of the mid-century. Apart from a small core of skilled labour, heavy industries only employed casual labour, which, otherwise, would have been under-employed during slack periods in the agricultural year. Consequently, it is thought to be unlikely that this would have had any positive or negative effect on the increasing levels of unemployment after 1550. The important consideration is that there was technical change, innovation, and diversification in this sector. This would provide a sound base for growth in the second half of the century.

* The area that is seen as making a positive contribution to economic growth between 1350 and 1550 is the rural textile industry. Until the thirteenth century England was a backward offshore island in economic terms, exporting raw materials such as wool, leather and tin to the more advanced continent. Manufacturing was largely confined to the towns and was controlled by the craft guilds. Levels of production were low, which made the finished articles expensive. These manufactures were either sold locally through the town markets, or distributed more widely through the system of international fairs which stretched right across western Europe. The restrictive practices of the guilds and the high cost of living in towns (see page 12) made expansion difficult. For this reason many craftsmen in the textile trades left the towns during the thirteenth century to set up new industry in the countryside.

Historians have various explanations for this development, but it is widely agreed that the main motive was to escape high urban costs and to utilise the cheap, surplus rural labour force. This is the origin of the theory of proto-industrialisation. Advocates of this theory point out that in every peasant society there is a certain amount of cottage industry, because most peasant families have to supplement their incomes with wages. Crafts such as spinning, weaving, glove and basket-making were carried out by peasant families in their own cottages. It was these skills that the new rural clothmakers were anxious to utilise. The significance of this form of textile manufacture was that it was large-scale, and exported increasing quantities of semi-finished cloth to the continent, which was economically more advanced than just exporting raw wool.

*Until the middle of the sixteenth century this cottage (or putting-out) industry was organised by clothiers. Raw materials such as wool or yarn were purchased by the clothier, who distributed them to his workforce for manufacturing in their cottages using their own tools. This is seen as a significant division of labour because the various stages of manufacture were separated, and only the clothiers sold the completed piece of cloth. It also meant that the clothier had no large outlay to provide buildings or equipment, as was the case in heavy industry. The only high cost buildings required were the water-driven fulling mills to felt and thicken the woollen cloth by shrinking and rolling it so that the fibres interlocked, and in most cases existing flour mills could be used for this purpose. The capital costs were the purchase of the raw materials and the wages for the workforce. However, until the middle of the sixteenth century it is thought that many of the cottage workforce, particularly the weavers, remained self-employed, and were not entirely dependent on wages. The development of a major exporting industry in England is considered to be a significant economic advance, and to have marked the beginning of capitalistic manufacture. The main areas of clothmaking were East Anglia, the West Country, and parts of Yorkshire. In Norfolk fine worsteds were produced, while in the other areas the main products were the highly-prized broadcloths (12 yards by 1.75 yards) and the cheaper, but popular, kerseys (18 yards by 1 yard). Because the English dyeing and finishing trades were technically inferior to those on the continent, the cloth was exported undyed, and semi-finished. This 'white' cloth was finished and dyed on the continent, particularly in the Netherlands, and was then sold by foreign merchants.

Although the rural textile industry is seen as the major contributor to England's economic growth up to 1550, it did create a number of problems. As the putting-out system was free of guild regulations it was not necessary for those taking part in it to have served an apprenticeship. This meant that gentry, yeomen and prosperous husbandmen could set themselves up as clothiers, which caused resentment among the members of the town guilds who saw it as unfair competition. Marxist historians see this as part of the conflict caused by the transition from feudalism to capitalism; a clash between small-scale, feudalistic guild manufacture, and large-scale capitalistic production. Many other economic historians consider that the rivalry was caused by the government's failure to enforce regulations in the countryside.

Whichever explanation is accepted it is clear that by the early sixteenth century the gentry, yeomen and husbandmen had established a variety of rural industries such as textiles, leather crafts and stocking knitting, which competed with the more expensive products of the urban guilds. From the beginning of the sixteenth century the government repeatedly passed legislation to try to exert greater control over rural industry. In part this was in response to complaints about shoddy workmanship and poor quality goods levelled at the putting-out industry by the towns. At the same time the State was trying to take greater control over the economy in general.

An Act Touching Weavers 1555

1 Foreasmuch as the weavers of this realm have, as well at this present parliament as at divers other times, complained that the rich and wealthy clothiers do many ways oppress them, some by setting up and keeping in their houses divers looms,
5 and keeping and maintaining them by journeymen and persons unskilful, to the decay of a great number of artificers which were brought up in the said science of weaving . . . It is therefore, for remedy of the premises, and for avoiding of a great number of inconveniences which may grow, ordained,
10 established and enacted, by authority of this present parliament, that no person using the feat or mystery of clothmaking, and dwelling out of a city, borough, market town or corporate town, shall . . . keep, retain or have in his or their house or possession any more or above one woollen loom at one time . . .

Passed in 1555, the Act Touching Weavers, like its predecessors, proved ineffectual, and it was not until 1563 that the government finally began. to exercise some control over rural cloth manufacture. The reason for this success in the 1560s may well have been that by then the textile industry was in the process of a drastic reorganisation. During the 1550s textile exports had slumped, and the production of the 'old draperies' collapsed. Clothmakers had to adjust to demand for a different type of textile, the 'new draperies'. Eventually English manufacturers, with the help of emigrants from the continent, mastered the new techniques, and a renewed export boom began.

However, in the 1550s the effect was disastrous. Attempts by the authorities to remedy the situation were generally crude and heavy-handed. In 1559 William Cecil was suggesting the restoration of the unpopular Vagrancy Act of 1547 (see page 31). Furthermore he recommended that servants and labourers should not be allowed to leave their villages, and no one should be apprenticed unless his father

---

Enactment of the Common Council of London as to the Age of
ending Apprenticeship 1556

1 For as much as great poverty, penury, and lack of living hath
of late years followed . . . and one of the chieftest occasions
thereof, as it is thought . . . is by the over hasty marriages and
over soon setting up of households of and by youth and young
5 folks of the same city . . . for remedy, stay, and reformation
whereof it is ordained . . . that no manner of persons . . . shall
be any manner of ways or means made free of the said city . . .
until such time as he and they shall severally attain to the age of
24 years.

---

was a gentleman or merchant, and owned land worth at least ten
pounds a year.

*Historians have no difficulty in identifying the causes of the
widespread destitution in the textile trades and in the towns. The long
period of growth in cloth exports had ended, so bringing a sustained
period of economic growth from the 1460s to an abrupt halt. It is agreed
that the basic cause of this problem was the collapse of the Antwerp
cloth market, but there were a number of contributory factors, all of
which need to be considered to understand the economic difficulties in
mid-Tudor England.

The underlying problem can be traced to developments in the
fifteenth century. By the 1440s textile exports had risen to some 55,000
cloths a year, while wool exports had fallen to an annual 9,000 sacks. In
the middle of the century trade was adversely affected by the general
western European trade recession, following the population losses
resulting from the Black Death and subsequent plague cycle. At the
same time England was in a weak diplomatic position after the loss of
the war with France and the beginning of the Wars of the Roses.
Consequently, English merchants lost control of their markets in
central Europe and the Baltic to their main commercial rivals, the
German merchants of the Hanseatic League. When trade recovered in
the 1460s, almost half the English cloth exports were controlled by the
Hanse, and other foreign merchants. At the same time the English
share of the trade had become monopolised by the Merchant Adventurers, who were a powerful group of traders drawn mainly from the
London Livery Companies. They owed their dominant position to the
large loans which they gave to the Crown, in return for which they were
granted privileges over other English merchants. Driven out of other
continental markets, the Merchant Adventurers established themselves
at Antwerp in the Netherlands.

This was to have a number of important consequences for English
trade up to the 1550s. The Netherlands was a major centre for the

dyeing and finishing of cloth, and this made it very convenient for the export of English 'white' textiles. Furthermore, at the time of the Merchant Adventurers' removal to Antwerp, the city was becoming the main commercial and financial centre in western Europe. This created what is known as the Antwerp-London 'funnel'. The monopoly of the Merchant Adventurers meant that English cloth exports came to be channelled through London, which controlled 90 per cent of the trade by the 1550s. At the same time English imports of wine, spices, manufactured goods and luxury items became concentrated on Antwerp. One beneficial effect of this commercial axis was that by the middle of the sixteenth century some 70 per cent of the country's overseas trade was controlled by English merchants. On the other hand, English ports such as Bristol, York, Hull and Southampton declined, and many merchants outside London complained that they were being excluded from the continental market.

The link with Antwerp created a variety of problems through its very success. Cloth exports had risen from some 40,000 cloths a year in the late fifteenth century, to 130,000 a year in the 1540s. At the same time exports of tin, leather and hides rose, and the volume of imports increased. Although this is considered to show notable economic growth, the market was not very stable. There were sudden slumps in demand, such as in the 1520s, which caused widespread unemployment in textile manufacturing areas. Much of the rise in the volume of exports in the 1540s was the result of the repeated debasement of the English coinage. This, by reducing the value of sterling against continental currencies, artificially stimulated demand for English goods abroad by making them cheaper, and so made the slump after 1550 even deeper. The importance of the trade to both England and the Netherlands made it a pawn in diplomatic exchanges and foreign policy. The early Tudors frequently used the threat of withholding cloth exports to try to force the Habsburg Empire into wars against France. Such a policy finally helped to bring about the collapse of Antwerp when relationships with Charles V broke down during Northumberland's temporary alliance with France in 1550 (see page 56). Both sides placed restrictions on trade, and this forced English merchants to begin to look for new markets.

Although the Antwerp market did not finally collapse until the 1570s, its preceding decline left English trade in a very exposed position. During the first half of the sixteenth century the volume of exports to Antwerp had made English merchants disinclined to seek out alternative markets. In spite of advice, such as that given by Robert Thorne in his book *Declaration of the Indes*, very little effort was made to establish new trade outlets within Europe, or elsewhere in the world. It was not until the initial slump in the trade to the Netherlands in the early 1550s that the Privy Council and the London merchants began to promote exploration in the search for new markets. The establishment of the Muscovy Company in 1554 (see page 58) was the first step in this direction. In any case, the underlying cause of the decline of the Antwerp market was the change in the pattern of demand. Both European and colonial buyers began to favour lighter types of fabric made of silk, cotton, or linen mixed with wool, instead of the heavy woollen cloth of the 'old draperies'. This meant that the English economy during the second half of the sixteenth century not only had to find alternative markets, but, also, to restructure to meet the technical demands of the 'new draperies'.

*The levels of unemployment in the 1550s were made worse by what many historians regard as an 'urban crisis'. In some, but not all respects this is considered to be a consequence of the development of the rural textile industry. The first stage of urban decline came from the effects of competition from the more cost-effective putting-out system. Then, in the fifteenth century, towns were adversely affected by the population losses caused by the Black Death and the continued influence of the plague cycle. Urban populations declined rapidly, especially because their crowded living conditions produced higher mortality rates. The situation was made worse because the fall in overall population drastically reduced the flow of migrants needed to maintain, or increase, the number of town dwellers. When population levels began to recover during the first half of the sixteenth century, the situation was reversed. Towns faced the problem of having to house, feed and employ large numbers of young and generally unskilled migrants from the countryside. At the same time, town guilds had to meet growing competition from the rural industries. It was this situation which forced early Tudor governments to try to legislate in favour of urban manufacturing.

Although the concept of an urban crisis is quite attractive – and many towns did suffer a severe decline – this can be regarded as part of the natural pattern of urban recession and recovery. While some towns went into temporary eclipse, others actually expanded. In any case the picture is distorted by the abnormal expansion of London. Between 1500 and 1560 the population of London is estimated to have risen from 50,000 to 90,000. By comparison the population of Norwich, the second largest town, is considered to have remained virtually static at 12,000 over the same period. In part this is a reflection of the influence of London's monopoly of the Antwerp trade. Possibly of equal importance was that London was becoming recognised as the centre of government and the capital of England. Although the rapid expansion of London did undoubtedly cast a temporary blight over many of the other towns, urban historians tend to see this as a highly significant development. London's emergence as a capital city is regarded as an engine for economic growth by the end of the sixteenth century.

*As in the case of the agricultural sector, there is no clear evidence of an industrial or commercial crisis in the mid-sixteenth century.

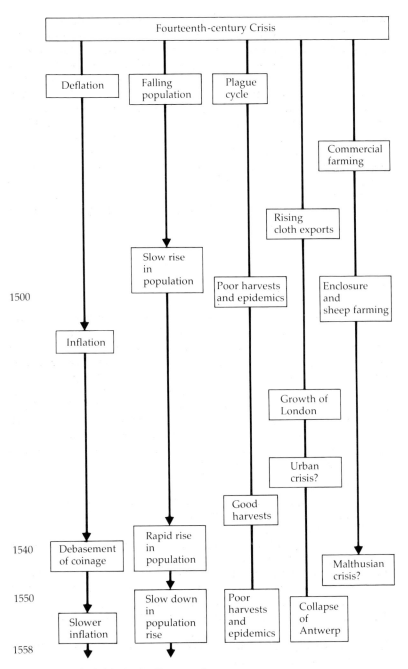

Summary – A Crisis in the Economy?

Although cloth exports were becoming unstable by 1549 there is no real sign that unemployment added to the popular discontent in that year. By the 1550s unemployment was becoming a problem in many towns, but most of the rural textile workers had other occupations and the produce of their cottage gardens to fall back on. This is not to say that there was not widespread hardship in many areas. However, it must be remembered that during the 1550s the level of population was actually falling, and this might account for the lack of discontent in spite of the run of very bad harvests. Most economic historians see the mid-sixteenth century as the end of a period of growth which had begun during the late fifteenth century. During that time industry had become more efficient, and was beginning to catch up with continental technology. By the 1550s the economy in general is seen as having achieved a firm foundation on which future economic growth could be based.

Making notes on 'A Crisis in the Economy?'

Your notes should help you to decide how far the English economy had evolved towards capitalism by the middle of the sixteenth century. Clearly there were problems of different kinds in all sectors of the economy. You have to make up your mind about how important these difficulties were, and whether they amounted to a crisis. You will also need to think carefully about how the economy affected all the other aspects of life in England, and to what extent it created problems. Equally you need to familiarise yourself with the way in which historians look at the economy, and remember the difficulties they have in coming to any firm conclusions. The following headings and questions should help you decide what notes to make:

1. Introduction.
1.1. How do economic historians interpret economic change?
1.2. What are the different theories of economic change in the early sixteenth century?
1.3. What are the difficulties in interpreting the commercialisation of the agricultural and industrial sectors?
1.4. How do historians interpret the commercialisation of world trade?
1.5. What are the problems of interpreting the historical evidence?
2. Population, Inflation and the Standard of Living.
2.1. Why is there so much debate over population increase between the 1470s and the 1520s?
2.2. What are the difficulties of measuring population growth between the 1520s and the 1550s?
2.3. Why were there such variations in the rate of population recovery?

2.4. What evidence is there for over-population and grain shortages by 1550?

2.5. What were the causes of inflation up to the 1550s?

2.6. How might rent and wage levels have added to popular discontent?

2.7. Why might 1549 be regarded as a particularly bad year?

3. Agriculture.

3.1. What are the main debates over early sixteenth-century agriculture?

3.2. Why was agriculture unable to support a population of six million by 1300, and how did the situation change in the fifteenth century?

3.3. What problems were caused by the presence of different farming regions?

3.4. Why do some historians think that there was an agricultural revolution in sixteenth-century England? Why do other historians disagree with this theory?

3.5. Why are enclosures thought to have created grain shortages by 1549?

3.6. Why might farming specialisation have caused problems of food supply by 1549?

4. Industry, Commerce and the Urban Crisis.

4.1. What are the main debates over early sixteenth-century industry?

4.2. Why do historians disagree over a possible industrial revolution in sixteenth-century England?

4.3. What were the main changes in heavy industry and how did they influence the economy?

4.4. How do historians explain the expansion of the rural textile industry, and why was the change significant?

4.5. How was the rural textile industry organised? What problems did it create?

4.6. What caused the slump in textile exports, and what were the consequences?

4.7. What are the arguments for and against there being an 'urban crisis' in the first half of the sixteenth century?

Answering essay questions on 'A Social and Economic Crisis, 1547–58?'

As no doubt you will have understood from reading the chapters on social change and economic change, the issues that have particularly interested historians on these aspects of the topic have a timescale that extends beyond the reigns of Edward and Mary. This pattern of historical research tends to be reflected in the questions examiners choose to ask. So it is unlikely that you will ever be asked to write an entire essay on either social or economic change in the mid-century period. You are much more likely to be invited to discuss social and/or economic change over a wider period, to include social and economic factors within a general essay on the mid-century period, or (rarely) to combine social and economic issues in an answer restricted to the years 1547 to 1558.

Consider the following questions and assign them to the three categories described in the previous sentence:

1. '"The English economy in 1600 was essentially the English economy of 1500." Discuss this assessment of economic development in sixteenth-century England.'
2. 'How far was there a social and economic crisis during the reigns of Edward VI and Mary I?'
3. 'Was England close to revolution in 1549?'
4. 'Assess the achievements of the Duke of Northumberland between 1549 and 1553.'
5. 'What were the effects of inflation in England between 1500 and 1558?'
6. 'To what extent were the élites under threat in mid-sixteenth-century England?'

It should be possible to answer the second question from what you have learnt from the previous two chapters. This is a straightforward 'How far/to what extent?' type of question. What would be the two main parts of your answer to this question? This is a good example of a question that lends itself to the inclusion of the differing views of historians – a dimension to an answer that is often highly rewarded by examiners. This approach could even be built into the basic plan for the answer, which could revolve around two ideas – 'historians used to think that ...' and 'historians now generally agree that ...' Complete each of these ideas, and then draw up a detailed plan for answering question 2 using this approach. Which idea would you present first? Why?

Source-based questions on 'A Crisis in the Economy?'

1 Changes in agriculture
Read the extract from Sir Thomas Smith's *A Discourse on the Commonweal of this Realm of England* (1549), given on page 128. Answer the following questions:
a) What is the meaning of 'dearth' (line 5)? (1 mark)
b) What does the husbandman suggest were the incentives to enclose land? (2 marks)

c) What does the husbandman suggest was the reason why more land in his village was not enclosed? (2 marks)
d) What were the consequences of enclosure as reported by the husbandman? What other consequences of enclosure caused anxiety among the authorities at the time? (6 marks)
e) Who gained and who lost from sixteenth-century enclosures? (4 marks)

2   Attempts to reduce urban unemployment
Read the extract from An Act Touching Weavers (1555), given on page 134, and the Enactment of the Common Council of London as to the Age of ending Apprenticeship (1556), given on page 135. Answer the following qustions:
a) In the first extract, what is the meaning of (i) 'brought up in' (line 7), and (ii) 'feat or mystery' (line 11)? (2 marks)
b) What were the Act and the Enactment attempting to achieve? In each case how was it intended to achieve the desired end? (6 marks)
c) What was the stated reason for attempting to limit the number of rural looms? Was this likely to have been the real reason? Explain your answer. (3 marks)
d) Were the Act and the Enactment likely to have been successful in achieving their intended outcomes? Why was this? (6 marks)
e) What do these extracts indicate about the expectations the author- ities had of themselves in the mid-sixteenth century? (3 marks)

CHAPTER 7

Conclusion

Since the 1970s historians have paid great attention to the emergence of capitalism in early modern England. This has resulted in considerable debate among writers of all shades of opinion. Generally this has been set within the context of the transition from feudalism to capitalism. Such a transition is not just seen as a change in economic organisation, but as a rearrangement of political, social, economic and cultural relationships. Within the overall concept of such a transition new general theories, such as the rise of the State or the rise of the world system, have been created. At the same time existing theories, such as the rise of the gentry and the rise of the bourgeoisie, have been carefully re-examined. This whole process of change and continuity was seen to be punctuated by crises in particular areas of the State, society, and the economy. At times, it was considered, these merged into a general western European crisis, notably in the fourteenth and early seventeenth centuries. England, it was thought, might have experienced a separate crisis of its own in the mid-sixteenth century. Recently historians have begun to attach less importance to such a broad theoretical approach, because history, unlike science or the social sciences, is now seen to be less easy to define in terms of general laws. Historians agree that general theories are useful in organising the great mass of historical events into a manageable and understandable form. However, it is being increasingly realised that such generalisation obscures more than it reveals. While models are still felt to be helpful in promoting investigation and stimulating debate, historical research is becoming more focused at a regional, county and parish level. It is hoped that these studies, by revealing the infinite variety of events and experiences of people in the past, will help to deepen our understanding of them.

The concept of a mid-sixteenth-century crisis in England is now considered to be difficult to maintain. This is certainly true if by 'crisis' it is implied that the whole of the country, and all the people, were experiencing a crisis continuously between 1547 and 1558. Indeed, it is only really possible to say that the country as a whole and some sections of society underwent very short-lived crises at times between these dates. If this is the case, most historians would consider that this was normal for any country at any time. Mid-Tudor England faced a variety of problems. Many of these arose from the political, social and economic consequences of the feudal crisis. Others, like the reactions to the English Reformation, can be seen as more short-term. A few, such as the succession crisis of 1553, were responses to immediate events. At no time, even in 1549, was the country in danger of collapse, and for most people life went on as normal.

*Some historians attach great importance to the potential constitutional and political crisis arising from Henry VIII's inability to provide an adult male heir. With the anarchy of the Wars of the Roses still very much a living memory there were obvious fears that the Tudor State would collapse into chaos. Such worries proved to be groundless. The permanent machinery of state continued to function without a break after 1547, showing that the 'revolution in government' under the first two Tudor monarchs had achieved a firm basis. At the same time the élites provided great support and loyalty to the legitimate monarchy. Although there was considerable rivalry between the political factions under Edward VI, it was no greater than it had been during the reign of Henry VIII. At no time, even in 1549 with the fall of Somerset, was there a real political crisis. The most dangerous moment came in 1553 with the death of Edward VI, when Northumberland tried to bar Princess Mary from the succession. Once again the élites were solid in their support for the legitimate descent, and the incident passed without crisis. It is true that the political leadership was often inept and indecisive between 1547 and 1558. Even so the structure of the administration continued to function without a check, and some useful measures of bureaucratic reform were passed. When Mary I died in 1558 the Crown was offered peacefully to her sister Elizabeth, a tribute to the strength of Tudor government.

Although there is general agreement among historians that there was no serious mid-century political or constitutional crisis, opinions about the political leadership continue to vary. The 'good' Duke of Somerset is now seen in a much less favourable light, while the 'bad' Duke of Northumberland is credited with being a much more able politician than was previously thought. Mary I is still regarded as a monarch without any real ability, but her reign is now thought to have achieved some significant advances. Speculation about the true nature of Mary's personality continues, and doubtless future research will lead to further modifications in the assessment of these major political figures. At the same time great interest is being shown in the nature of the ruling élites in general. New analyses of the nobility and the gentry, both at national and county levels, are being produced. Particular attention is being paid to the study of individual families and their circle of friends and associates, to reveal the part they played in local and central government. Such research should lead to a much greater understanding of the complex motives and ambitions behind the political factions of mid-Tudor England.

*The lack of political leadership between 1547 and 1558 placed England in a weak diplomatic position in foreign affairs. However, in no way did this amount to a crisis, as the country was never in real danger of foreign invasion. Moreover, it is unlikely that even strong leadership would have improved the diplomatic situation. Mid-century foreign policy was largely dictated by relatively long-term processes –

the culmination of the Valois-Habsburg rivalry, and the tactics of Henry VIII. Somerset and Northumberland inherited a war against France and Scotland which Henry VIII to all intents and purposes had already lost. Faced with an impossible military situation and a bankrupt Exchequer, Northumberland's decision to make peace in 1550 was sensible, even if it was unpopular. Mary I's deep Catholic convictions and her attachment to Philip II of Spain made it almost inevitable that she would support the Habsburgs in the final, indecisive stage of the Habsburg-Valois wars, which ended in 1558. The loss of Calais severed England's final link with the continent. When Elizabeth came to the throne she was faced with a completely different diplomatic situation.

Mid-Tudor foreign policy is still seen as being largely dictated by the broader aims of western European diplomacy which had dominated the first half of the sixteenth century. England's diplomatic position was further complicated by fears over the succession and religious reform. In the past, historians made considerable use of official papers and the correspondence between ambassadors and their courts to reconstruct events and policies. More recently they have begun to think that over-reliance on this type of evidence produced a one-sided view of the issues. Official documents only state what governments wish to be left on record, while the views of ambassadors like Renard (the accredited representative of the Holy Roman Empire in England) are bound to be partisan. For this reason, much greater attention is being paid to the correspondence and family papers of the many lesser diplomats involved in foreign affairs. These men were drawn from a wide range of families among the élites, and such research increases not only the understanding of the intricate nature of diplomacy, but, also, its relationship with domestic politics. However, it is still unlikely that historians will be able to probe much deeper than the official versions of the growing number of plots and intrigues with foreign powers, because families were very careful to destroy such incriminating evidence.

*It is difficult to assess the impact of religious reform because the English Reformation was too close for either its long or even short-term effects to be really felt by the middle of the century. Clearly religion had immediate consequences for politics and foreign policy, but in neither case can it be said to have caused a crisis. The longer-term influences of social and economic change were only to become apparent during the next 100 years. It is now suggested that there was a great deal of religious compromise among the élites, and apathy, or even indifference, among the mass of the population towards religious change between 1547 and 1558. Zealous Catholics or Protestants were a small minority, and most people were prepared to tolerate the sudden switches of religious policy that occurred in the middle of the century. It is difficult to decide whether the religious uprising in the West Country was atypical. Possibly the western rebels, like their Norfolk counterparts, were indulging in nostalgia, and protesting for what they saw as better times in the past. Certainly the majority of the people of England were ready to accept the return of Protestantism under Elizabeth I.

There is still considerable disagreement among historians as to the true state of religion in mid-Tudor England. Although the course of religious change is well documented at the national level, it is still not clear whether Catholicism was maintaining, or Protestantism gaining, the support of the laity. While the loyalty of the Howard family for the Catholic faith, and the active patronage of Protestantism by the dowager Duchess of Suffolk are well documented, much less is known about the many uncommitted élite families. The growing volume of research into such families and their circle of friends is beginning to reveal more about the complexity of the motives governing political and religious alliances. It is a much greater problem to determine the attitudes of the ordinary people. A great deal of research is being carried out at county and parish level, but all this has revealed so far is that most people were prepared to conform by attending the services of the official religion. At present this is being interpreted as showing apathy and indifference towards religion. However, many historians still consider that attendance at church merely shows that the lower orders were deferring to their superiors. What needs to be known, if that is ever possible, is how ordinary people actually felt about religion, and what form of religious devotion they followed in the privacy of their own homes.

* The process of social change, although complicated and controversial, is easier to discern. The structure of society had evolved and diversified during the 200 years following the feudal crisis. Both the élites and the lower orders had been affected by change. Among the élites the emergence of the gentry from the ranks of the feudal aristocracy is seen as the most significant development. By the middle of the century the new structure had been strengthened by the sale of monastic and other church lands. Among the lower orders there had been considerable change over the same period. The servile, feudal peasantry had disappeared, to be replaced by a new hierarchy of yeomen, husbandmen, cottagers and labourers. Although a great gulf existed between the élites and the non-élites, the majority of the lower orders were freer and more prosperous than they had been 200 years before. By the middle of the sixteenth century there seems to have been considerable social stability, and little sign of social crisis. It was over the next century, when society began to evolve still further, that real signs of social disruption began to emerge.

Although the actual process of structural change is relatively easy to discern, it is much harder to decide what was actually happening below the surface. Mid-sixteenth-century England was still an unruly nation, and violence was present at all levels of society. The government and the élites expected and feared outbreaks of popular rioting during the summer months as part of the normal course of events. These might be sparked off by village sports or quarrels between neighbours, and a bad harvest, local enclosure, or unpopular taxation might cause widespread disorder, as in 1549. Nevertheless, there appears to have been a considerable degree of cooperation between social groups, particularly at local levels. The growing number of county studies and the research into gentry and noble families is revealing the diverse motives governing social relationships among the élites, and their attitudes towards the lower orders. The lack of evidence makes it harder to investigate opinions among the non-élites themselves. However, the official keeping of parish registers after 1538, and the growing number of wills and inventories left by people of relatively low social status helps historians to gain an insight into the lives of the ordinary people. Considerable attention is now being given to the study of popular culture and disorder, and in particular to the family and the role of women in society.

*The English economy had been similarly evolving for some 200 years. Agriculture had become more efficient through enclosures, specialisation, and commercial farming. However, because of over-concentration on wool and other animal products, it was barely able to feed the increased population by 1550; a problem which was to be overcome in the next century. There was a similar amount of change in the industrial sector. Heavy industry was still in the process of catching up with continental technology. The rural textile industry suffered temporary collapse in the 1550s after 100 years of economic growth, but was already adapting to new demands by the second half of the century. The slump in the Antwerp cloth market in the 1550s had forced English merchants to begin to seek new markets in Europe, and to take an interest in world trade. The restructuring of the agricultural and industrial sectors clearly caused some economic problems. However, it is doubtful that these amounted to a crisis. Nor does it seem that the rise in population and inflation in the first half of the sixteenth century, which helped economic expansion, created more than passing problems by the middle of the century. It appears that by the 1550s the English economy was in a relatively healthy condition, and prepared for another period of economic growth.

The increasing use of the computer and quantitative methods have enabled economic historians to establish the broad trends of population growth, fluctuations in wages, inflation, and the pattern of imports and exports more firmly. However, it is considered by many historians that historical sources are too fragmentary and unreliable for quantitative analysis to produce results of any real accuracy. In any case it is thought that too much attention has been given to examining economic processes to explain the industrial revolution of the nineteenth century, and that more attention should be given to detail. Recent research is being directed towards investigating the great diversity within the

English economy, rather than just measuring general growth and decline. Here again the work on gentry and noble families aids an understanding of their economic attitudes. This will possibly help to determine whether the current belief that the élites were more interested in buying land and building mansions than in investing in the economy, is actually true. At the same time more attention is being given to the development of regional and local markets and industry to see how they contributed to the national economy.

*If there was a crisis in the mid-sixteenth century it was in 1549, and was created by a range of misfortunes. There was a weak, insolvent government, over-stretching its resources by trying to fight a war on two fronts. Moreover, the government was attempting to introduce drastic religious reforms, and aroused the hostility of the élites and non-élites by its social and economic policies. By 1549 the population, which had been rising rapidly for the last decade, was peaking at around three million. Prices, fuelled by currency debasements and increasing population levels, had doubled since the beginning of the century. A run of good growing seasons came to an end, possibly because of a deterioration in the weather, and the harvest in 1549 was poor. This came at a time when agriculture was already struggling to feed the higher level of population, and so grain prices rose. Under these circumstances it is not surprising that underlying discontent came to the surface in the form of popular rebellions. Even so, if Somerset had not been unwilling to withdraw troops from Scotland and France, and if there had not been a power struggle developing in the Privy Council, it is unlikely that the situation would have got out of hand. Once the government had mobilised sufficient troops, the rebellions were suppressed with comparative ease. It must be considered that, if this was the worst that could happen in a particularly bad year, there is little reason to see the mid-century as a period of crisis.

Making notes on 'Conclusion'

This chapter reconsiders the issues raised in Chapter 1, and in particular assesses the question as to whether there was a mid-Tudor crisis. At the same time it examines the attitudes among historians towards the concept of crises in the past, and reviews some of the major trends of historical research into this period. You must think carefully about whether the idea of a mid-century crisis is useful in interpreting this period of Tudor history. Your notes should set out the arguments for and against a crisis, and indicate the direction of current historical research. The following questions should help you:

1.1. What are the arguments against using general historical theories, and what is the case against the concept of a mid-Tudor crisis?
1.2. What is the evidence against a political and constitutional crisis, and how are historians revising their views about the major political figures?
1.3. Why is it considered that there was no real diplomatic crisis, and what new types of evidence are historians using to revise their opinions?
1.4. Why is it so difficult to assess the part played by religion in mid-Tudor England, and how are historians trying to make the situation clearer?
1.5. What is the evidence against there being a social crisis, and what new approaches are being used by social historians?
1.6. Why did the problems in the economy not amount to a crisis, and why are historians becoming wary of quantitative methods?
1.7. In spite of its particular difficulties, why is the year 1549 still not regarded as one of crisis?

Answering essay questions on 'Edward VI and Mary: A Mid-Tudor Crisis?'

Re-read the 'Answering essay questions' section at the end of Chapter 1 (page 19). From it you will learn that this section is designed to assist you in answering questions that relate to more than one aspect of the topic over either a part or the whole of the period 1547–58.

Study the following questions. Divide them into the four main categories of essay questions ('What?', 'Why?', 'How far/to what extent?' and 'challenging statement').

1. 'Why was Mary I so unpopular among her subjects at the time of her death?'
2. ' "It was inevitable that the accession of a minor would lead to instability in the years after Henry VIII's death." Discuss.'
3. 'What were the implications of the Duke of Northumberland's failure to ensure the succession of Lady Jane Grey to the throne on the death of Edward VI in 1553?'
4. 'What were the causes of Mary I's failure to win the support of her people?'
5. 'Is the Duke of Northumberland's bad reputation justified?'
6. ' "The changes introduced by the central government during the reigns of Edward VI and Mary were largely cosmetic." Do you agree?'
7. 'How far is it fair to claim that "England suffered from poor leadership in the years between the death of Henry VIII and the accession of Elizabeth I"?'

The only question that does not obviously fit into one of the four categories is question 5. Yet a little thought should lead to the conclusion that it is essentially a 'How far/to what extent?' type of question. In fact, if the words 'How far' had been included at the beginning of the question, the best way of answering it would remain the same. In either case a two-part answer – 'to this extent yes' and 'to this extent no' – is called for.

Questions 1 to 4 are virtually identical. What differences should there be in the way they are answered? In practice, there are likely to be none of significance. This is because 'why' and 'what were the causes' are sufficiently synonymous for it to be possible to claim that both questions are 'why?' category questions. This is yet further evidence of the need to read questions for meaning rather than to pick out what appear to be the key words – which, as you know, can be very misleading.

Of course, reading questions for meaning is much more than just decoding the examiner's intentions. A vital part of the process is the identification of the dubious assumptions that are lurking in many questions. The questions above contain many such dubious assump-

	1547–9	1549–53	1553–8
Domestic politics			
Foreign affairs			
Religion			
Society			
The economy			

tions. Make a list of them, starting with the assumption in question 1 that Mary was 'so unpopular'. Better candidates often comment briefly on these questionable assumptions in the introduction to their essay. In the case of the first question it would be a matter of explaining that, although Mary was widely unpopular, she was not universally so. What is the assumption in the fifth question? It might need to be discussed at greater length than normal, possibly even having a paragraph devoted to it in your plan. Certainly it deserves more than a passing reference.

In order to be well prepared to answer questions such as question 5, you need to have your information arranged chronologically as well as by aspect (following the pattern of this book). The most manageable way in which to do this is by completing a matrix (but with much larger boxes) such as the one opposite. Each entry should provide the date and the name of an important event. The creation of such a matrix would be a very useful revision exercise.

Further Reading

A great variety of books have been written about Tudor England, including some specifically on the mid-century period. Although you only have a relatively limited amount of time for additional reading, you should not be content to read general histories of the period, however good they are, but also try to look at some of the more specialist volumes. The following suggestions are representative of the different types of books available, and they have been selected because they are both readable and will give you the flavour of the range of interpretations of the period.

J. Guy, *Tudor England* (Clarendon, 1988)

This is the most recent general history and it will give you an insight into the latest research on and interpretation of the Tudor period. It also has useful chapters on the economy and society.

J. Loach and J. Tittler (eds.), *The Mid-Tudor Polity c.1540–1560* (Macmillan, 1980)

This is the best of the latest books on mid-Tudor England. It contains a range of interpretations by different historians, and is particularly useful on the reassessment of the Duke of Northumberland.

B. L. Beer, *Rebellion and Riot: Popular Disorder in England during the Reign of Edward VI* (Ohio, Kent State University Press, 1982) and
D. Loades, *The Reign of Mary Tudor: Politics, Government and Religion in England 1553–1558* (Ernest Benn, 1979)

These two books will give some very useful insights into how historians are now beginning to assess the reigns of Edward VI and Mary I.

D. C. Coleman, *The Economy of England 1450–1750* (OUP, 1977)

This is still the most readable book on the English economy. It gives a clear and uncomplicated explanation of the economy, and has many useful tables and graphs.

J. Youings, *Sixteenth Century England* (Penguin Books, 1984)

This is very well worth reading for a clear and informative insight into Tudor society. There is a full and informative bibliography.

I. Wallerstein, *The Modern World-System 1* (Academic Press, 1974)

For a very readable insight into the theoretical background and the key debates on the period this book is invaluable. There are very good chapters on the rise of the State, and on the debate about the rise of the gentry and the emergence of English capitalism.

Sources on Mid-Tudor England

There is a good range of accessible published primary material which includes coverage of the period 1547–58.

G. R. Elton, *The Tudor Constitution* (CUP, 1962)

This book is still the standard volume for constitutional and governmental papers.

M. Levine, *Tudor Dynastic Problems 1467–1571* (George Allen and Unwin, 1973)

This volume has a rather different selection of documents, and is particularly useful in gaining an insight into the problems of the Tudor succession.

A. Fletcher, *Tudor Rebellions* (Longman, 1968)

There is good coverage of the rebellions of 1549 from primary sources, although the analysis is now dated.

W. T. Sheils, *The English Reformation 1530–1570* (Longman, 1989)

This seminar book discusses recent interpretations of religious change and has a good documentary section.

H. E. S. Fisher and A. R. J. Jurica, *Documents in English Economic History from 1000–1760* (Bell and Sons, 1977)

This is now the standard source for economic documents.

J. M. Jack, *Trade and Industry in Tudor and Stuart England* (George Allen and Unwin, 1977)

This seminar book contains some useful discussion of approaches to economic history, and provides a range of alternative documentary sources.

Index